A Timely Encounter:

Nineteenth-Century Photographs of Japan

A TIMELY ENCOUNTER

Nineteenth-Century Photographs of Japan

An exhibition of photographs from the collections of the Peabody Museum
of Archaeology and Ethnology and the Wellesley College Museum

CONTRIBUTORS

Melissa Banta · Ellen Handy · Haruko Iwasaki · Bonnell D. Robinson

VOLUME EDITORS AND EXHIBITION CURATORS

Melissa Banta · Susan Taylor

PEABODY MUSEUM PRESS, CAMBRIDGE, MASSACHUSETTS · WELLESLEY COLLEGE MUSEUM, WELLESLEY, MASSACHUSETTS

The exhibition "A Timely Encounter: Nineteenth-Century Photographs of Japan" is organized by the Wellesley College Museum and the Peabody Museum, Harvard University, with the assistance of funds from the New England Foundation for the Arts, a private, non-profit organization developing and promoting the arts of the region. The New England Foundation for the Arts is sponsoring the exhibition's nation-wide tour.

The accompanying catalogue is funded by Konica Business Machines U.S.A., Inc., with additional funding provided by the Wellesley College Friends of Art and the Edwin O. Reischauer Institute of Japanese Studies.

ISBN 0–87365–810–8
Library of Congress Catalog Number: 88-60708

Printed in the United States of America

Photography by Hillel Burger
Design, printing, and binding by Meriden-Stinehour Press, Meriden, Connecticut and Lunenburg, Vermont
Editing by Donna Dickerson, Mary Strother, and Lucy Flint-Gohlke

Cover Illustration
Stillfried & Andersen Co. studio imprint, ca. 1880s
Albumen print (PM H15038)
Samurai warrior

Frontispiece Illustration
Studio unknown, ca. 1870s–1880s
Albumen print (WCM a1314)
Women laundering clothes

Contents

Preface 6

Curators' Note 6

Acknowledgments 7

Timetable of Historical Events 8

Timetable of Photographic Events 8

Life of a Photograph: 11
Nineteenth-Century Photographs of Japan
from the Peabody Museum and Wellesley
College Museum
MELISSA BANTA

Western Images, Japanese Identities: 23
Cultural Dialogue between East and West
in Yokohama Photography
HARUKO IWASAKI

Transition and the Quest for Permanence: 39
Photographers and Photographic Technology
in Japan, 1854–1880s
BONNELL D. ROBINSON

Tradition, Novelty, and Invention: 53
Portrait and Landscape Photography
in Japan, 1860s–1880s
ELLEN HANDY

Preface

The Wellesley College Museum and Peabody Museum are pleased to present *A Timely Encounter: Nineteenth-Century Photographs of Japan*. This joint exhibition was undertaken after the discovery that the collections of both museums not only contain fine examples of these hand-colored albumen photographs, all in pristine condition, but also complement each other well. The Peabody's strength is striking studio portraits while Wellesley's collection has many beautiful landscape scenes. They document a wide spectrum of Japanese life and culture, contributing to our understanding of this period in historical, photographic, anthropological, and art-historical terms. Renewed interest in these photographs for their aesthetic quality as well as for their documentary and historical value has prompted their re-examination. The programs offered by the Peabody Museum, a museum of archeology and ethnology, and the Wellesley College Museum, an art institution, reflect this dual nature.

The exhibition and accompanying catalogue, produced through the shared resources of the Wellesley College and Peabody museums, present four approaches to the study of these photographs. The first essay, by Melissa Banta, examines the history behind the collections. The role of the collectors William Sturgis Bigelow and Mary Alice Knox, responsible for the holdings at the Peabody and Wellesley College Museum respectively, is considered within the context of their interests and tastes. The second essay, by Haruko Iwasaki, places the emergence of photography in Japan within the country's changing social and cultural context before and after the Meiji Restoration of 1868. She examines the mutually influential relationship between Western and Japanese photographers and the complex cultural dialogue between Japan and the West in the second half of the nineteenth century. In the third essay, Bonnell Robinson outlines early photographers and photographic processes in Japan from the time of Commodore Perry's arrival until the late 1880s. She considers how photographers influenced by Western and Japanese cultures overcame technical and aesthetic challenges to express their respective visions of Japan. Finally, in the essay by Ellen Handy, the photographs are analyzed within the context of nineteenth-century European photography and art. She focuses specifically on the portrait and landscape genres, comparing and contrasting the Japanese photographs with Western conventions and pictorial methods.

While our gratitude toward the organizations and individuals who have generously supported the exhibition and publication is expressed in the Acknowledgments, we would like to especially thank Konica Business Machines U.S.A., Inc., for their generous support of the catalogue. We also extend our gratitude to Melissa Banta, Director of Photographic Archives at the Peabody Museum: her dedication to the project and remarkable ability to coordinate three scholars and two collections have indeed made the exhibition possible. Our thanks, too, to the three contributors to the catalogue, each of whom has brought a particular perspective to the project, which have combined to present a more complete portrayal of the characters, circumstances, and events of our timely encounter.

Susan M. Taylor
Director
Wellesley College Museum

C. C. Lamberg-Karlovsky
Director
Peabody Museum of
Archaeology and Ethnology,
Harvard University

Curators' Note

The lack of documentation for nineteenth-century photographs of Japan makes it difficult to accurately identify photographers. The majority of the Bigelow photographs in the Peabody collection bear on their mounts the imprint of the studio of Austrian photographer Baron Raimund Stillfried von Rathenitz, active in Japan from 1871–1885. A photographer's number, originally scratched onto the negative, appears on the Knox prints in the Wellesley collection. The handwriting style and range of numbers indicate that these photographs may also come from the Stillfried studio. Yet it is not possible to attribute each photograph to Stillfried or his studio assistants with assurance. In 1877 Stillfried took over the studio and the stock of negatives of the Venetian photographer Felice Beato; photographs taken by Beato may have been reprinted by Stillfried or his assistants, sometimes cropped and/or numbered. Some researchers have suggested that photographs appearing in the album Stillfried and Andersen prepared in 1877 that bear no number must be photographs by Beato; later versions of these same images often have a number added. A careful and systematic cataloguing of various versions of specific images, and comparison with verified attributions, remains to be undertaken. For the purposes of this exhibition and catalogue, no attribution has been made or accepted unless the photographer has been positively identified on the basis of documentary evidence available to the researchers.

The bibliographies in the catalogue are not comprehensive but document sources used in the preparation of the essays and provide references for the interested reader. The presentation of these images from the two collections clearly raises many more questions than can be answered at this time. We hope that the exhibition will stimulate further study of the complex and fascinating field of nineteenth-century photography in Japan.

Acknowledgments

This exhibition and catalogue, the result of a mutually enlightening collaboration between two institutions, was made possible through the contributions of many individuals and organizations. The project was funded by the New England Foundation for the Arts (NEFA), Konica Business Machines U.S.A., Inc., the Friends of Art of Wellesley College, and the Edwin O. Reischauer Institute of Japanese Studies. The New England Foundation for the Arts is sponsoring the exhibition's nationwide tour. To all of these organizations we extend our deepest thanks.

We would like to thank Janie Cohen, NEFA's former acting director of visual arts and media, who first suggested that the two institutions work together. Marilyn Weiss, current exhibitions coordinator for NEFA, has ably assisted us in every phase of the project.

At the Peabody Museum, director C. C. Lamberg-Karlovsky and assistant director Rosemary A. Joyce have provided kind encouragement and a continued commitment to bring the museum's photographic collections to a wide audience. Particular thanks go to Lea S. McChesney, administrator of exhibitions, for her assistance and guidance throughout the project. At the Wellesley College Museum, the efforts of assistant director Lucy Flint-Gohlke were critical to the project. Her editorial perspective and contributions are gratefully acknowledged.

The dedication and talents of the staff from both institutions are deeply appreciated. We are grateful to Mary Strother, managing editor, and Donna Dickerson, editorial assistant at the Peabody Museum, whose sensitivity and perspective made an invaluable contribution to the catalogue. Special recognition goes to Barbara Isaac, photographic coordinator, and Jacqui Hrivnak, research assistant at the Peabody Museum, for their unstinting support in all phases of research and production.

Richard Riccio, exhibit designer at the Peabody Museum, Kathleen Skelly, ethnographic specialist, and Richard Beauchamp, conservator, produced a thoughtful and elegant exhibition. We thank Robert Higgins, Wellesley College Museum preparator, for his efficiency and dedication. We are grateful for the skills of photographer Hillel Burger who made the fine reproductions for the catalogue and exhibition. Peabody and Wellesley registrars Genevieve Fisher and Jennifer Dowd Mason have expertly handled the exhibition's tour. We appreciate the support and advice of Daniel W. Jones, Jr., photographic archivist at the Peabody Museum.

Our thanks also go to Marjorie Dings, museum administrator at the Wellesley College Museum, and her assistant Sanda Boyd for their assistance in the planning and organization of the exhibition at Wellesley. The participation of Polly Giragosian, curatorial assistant at Wellesley, was critical to the success of the project. Marie Companion, slide curator at Wellesley, is also gratefully acknowledged for her assistance. Our thanks are extended as well to Wellesley College Museum student interns Debra Solomon and Lisa Downing for their help in preparing the manuscript. In addition, the efforts of C. Richard Bartels, C. Maile Black, Margaret Dubin, Una MacDowell, Ayano Ichida, Martha Lamberg-Karlovsky, Catherine Linardos, Joe Johns, Amy Raymond, John Thyng, Austin Brennan, Barbara Wiberg, H. Peter Szyszko and Beryl Noble at the Peabody Museum are warmly acknowledged.

The expertise of many individuals was important in the research of the two collections. In particular we would like to thank Maria Morris Hambourg at The Metropolitan Museum of Art, New York. We also thank Mack Lee and Julie Saul for their interest and assistance. Harold Rosin kindly provided information on attribution issues, and drew the curators' attention to an important catalogue Kusakabe Kimbei prepared of his own work. Advice on the collections was also generously given by Bill Johnston and Albert Craig at Harvard University. We are grateful to Patricia Berman at Wellesley College for her helpful and insightful observations.

Our deep appreciation goes to Henry Smith at the University of California at Santa Barbara and Izumi Shimada at Harvard University for their discerning criticism of the essays. Maureen Melton, archivist at the Boston Museum of Fine Arts, archivist Wilma Slaight and her assistant Carla Stewart at the Clapp Library at Wellesley College, and Kalman Applbaum and Fumiko Cranston at Harvard University graciously aided us in our research.

A number of museums and publishing companies cordially furnished us with additional images. We thank the Asian Art Museum of San Francisco, The Chrysler Museum, Harvard Arthur M. Sackler Museum, Harvard Fogg Art Museum, Harvard Widener Library, Harvard Tozzer Library, Honolulu Academy of Arts, The Japan Society of Northern California, Mondadori-Shueisha, Philadelphia Museum of Art, Wellesley College Archives, and Yokohama Archives of History. Benjamin LaFarge and Jack Naylor generously contributed prints from their private collections.

We were pleased to work with Meriden-Stinehour Press, and we extend our appreciation to Paul Hoffmann and David Hall for their expertise, which resulted in a finely produced catalogue. We thank Eric Harrington for the careful work he did in matting and framing the photographs.

The exhibition and catalogue are the result of the fine scholarship of Ellen Handy, Haruko Iwasaki, and Bonnell Robinson. They worked together sharing knowledge and diverse perspectives; individually their research has enhanced our understanding of these photographic collections and the time in history in which they were created. We thank each for contributing so generously to the project.

M.B. / S.T.

Timetable of Historical Events

Tokugawa Period (1600–1868)

1630s–1853 The Tokugawa Shogunate instituted a seclusion policy. International trade was limited to Dutch and Chinese traders in Nagasaki.

1800–1853 Tokugawa shogun's capital of Edo (Tokyo), with a population of over one million, had become the largest city in the world.

Economically, the western half of Honshū, Japan's main island, had grown increasingly prosperous, especially around Osaka and Kyoto. Northeastern Honshū experienced several famines, resulting in political unrest and numerous peasant uprisings.

Intellectually, the seclusion policy did not prevent the Japanese from studying Western medicine, astronomy, and military tactics through Dutch visitors, or from learning about the Napoleonic Wars in Europe and the Opium War in China. Meanwhile, National Learning (*Kokugaku*) became increasingly popular, fostering interest and pride in Japan's indigenous culture.

Bakumatsu (Latter Tokugawa) Period (1853–1868)

1853 Commodore Matthew C. Perry delivered a letter from President Millard Fillmore to the Tokugawa Shogunate demanding the opening of Japanese ports.

1854 The Treaty of Kanagawa opened the ports of Shimoda and Hakodate to foreign ships for supplies and repairs, but not trade.

1858 US–Japan Treaty of Amity and Commerce promised to open six ports to foreign trade, including Yokohama and Kobe, and granted the US extraterritorial rights, fixed tariff rates on imports, and most-favored nation status. Holland, Russia, Britain, and France soon signed similar treaties with the Tokugawa Shogunate.

The Tokugawa Shogunate's signing these treaties without imperial approval provoked political opposition and several incidents in which samurai opposed to Japan's opening attacked foreigners.

Revision of these "unequal treaties" became a central issue of government for the next forty years.

1858–1868 Because of the opening of Japan by the Tokugawa Shogunate, opposition to the shogunate became increasingly radical, especially among samurai from the domains of Satsuma and Chōshū. Following military defeats at the hands of Western powers in 1865, these two domains adopted Western-style military organizations and joined forces against the shogunate, which they overthrew in 1868 to reestablish imperial rule.

Meiji Period (1868–1912)

1869 Telegraph service between Tokyo and Yokohama was established.

1871 Domains governed by feudal lords and their samurai retainers were replaced by modern prefectures administered by governors and bureaucrats. In addition, the Tokugawa social class system, sword-carrying, and the traditional topknot were abolished.

1871–1872 Postal system was initiated. Railway between Shinbashi and Yokohama was opened.

1877 Failure of the Satsuma Rebellion ended the last vestiges of feudal resistance. Tokyo University was established, the outgrowth of a Tokugawa-period medical school.

1882–1887 Horse-tramways service began in Tokyo. The Tokyo Gas Company was inaugurated, and the city was lighted by electricity.

1890 Constitutional government was enacted under the Meiji Constitution.

Timetable of Photographic Events

1827 First permanent image produced by photochemical process by Joseph Nicéphore Nièpce in France.

1839 Daguerreotype process introduced by Louis Jacques Mandé Daguerre. Process utilized a silver-plated copper sheet and produced a unique single image.

1840 William Henry Fox Talbot introduced the first negative-to-positive process, which made the production of multiple prints possible. Paper negatives were used to make salt prints. The fibrous quality of the paper gave a soft appearance to the image.

1851–1885 Frederick Scott Archer introduced the collodion wet-plate process which used glass-plate negatives. The negatives yielded extremely sharp, finely detailed images with subtle gradations of tone.

1854 Commodore Matthew C. Perry was accompanied by daguerreotypist Eliphalet Brown, Jr., who documented the expedition to Japan.

1859 Shimooka Renjō, the first Japanese commercial photographer, opened his studio in Yokohama.

1850s–1860s By the late 1850s, photographic studios began to open in Japan. In the mid-1860s, the *Photo News* in London reported forty Japanese photographers in Osaka alone.

1850s–1890s The majority of photographs were printed on albumen paper. The egg-white emulsion secured a positive image on the surface of the paper and produced a glossy, grainless print which was toned to a rich brown.

1860 Ueno Hikoma bought a camera from a Dutch merchant and photographed various high ranking officials in Tokyo. He ran one of the most prestigious commercial photographic establishments in Nagasaki until the 1890s.

1861	J. G. Gower published the first commercially produced photographs of Japan in *Views of Japan*.
1862–1863	Felice Beato, an expeditionary photographer, opened a photographic studio in Yokohama.
1866	A fire destroyed most of Beato's early work.
1868	Beato's *Photographic Views of Japan* was published.
1870s	Pre-sensitized dry-plate collodion negatives, which had a faster emulsion than wet plates, became available. They could be processed long after the paper had been exposed to light and thus made photography a less cumbersome process.
1871	Baron Raimund Stillfried von Rathenitz established a studio in Yokohama and published *Views and Costumes of Japan*.
1873	The emperor and empress were photographed by Uchida Kuichi and the prints were distributed commercially.
1877	Stillfried bought out Beato's studio and stock.
1880	Gelatin silver prints were made available; they eventually overtook albumen prints on the market.
1880s	Ogawa Isshin became a successful society photographer. Kusakabe Kimbei bought out most of Stillfried's studio and operated his own firm until 1912. A. Farsari & Co. also acquired Stillfried's stock and operated one of Japan's largest commercial photographic firms.
1888	Introduction of the easy-to-operate, hand-held Kodak camera by George Eastman. Photography became more accessible to the amateur.
1889	William Kinnmond Burton was instrumental in founding the Japanese Photographic Society which became an immediate success.
1893	The Japanese Photographic Society sponsored the first International Photographic Exhibition in Japan.

2. Uchida Kuichi, Stillfried & Andersen Co. studio imprint, 1872
Hand-colored albumen print (PM H15041)
Mutsuhito, the Meiji Emperor, in Western military uniform.

3. Ichikawa Itoin, 1860
Wood-block print (Courtesy Jack Naylor Collection)

Westerners with a daguerreotype camera in a foreign settlement building in Yokohama.

In the early years of the new medium, photography was used to document cultural traditions at a time of unprecedented change in Japanese
society.

Life of a Photograph: Nineteenth-Century Photographs of Japan from the Peabody Museum and Wellesley College Museum

MELISSA BANTA

A photograph is at once a seemingly faithful mirror of reality and the product of an intrinsically subjective process. Beneath the reflection captured by the camera lies the intricate web of events surrounding the photograph's creation and use. It is in the unraveling of these events that the photograph's historical significance and elusive meanings come to light.

The photographs taken in nineteenth-century Japan that eventually made their way to Harvard's Peabody Museum and Wellesley College Museum collections have an interwoven and illuminating history. The story of their photographers, collectors, and eventual interpreters tells of a timely encounter between Western and Japanese cultures. Created at a moment of unprecedented change in Japanese society, these images capture cultural traditions and provide a hint of an emergent identity under the Meiji emperor. They reflect, as well, the vision and cultural attitudes of nineteenth-century photographers in Japan and the audiences they served. Finally, they are part of an ongoing process by which observers interpret another culture.

The Photographers and Their Subjects

The daguerreotype process heralded the beginning of photography in 1839. Recognized at its inception for its value as a documentary medium, photography was put to service on behalf of portraiture, land and architectural preservation, improvement of social conditions, and documentation of wartime ravages. Its invention coincided with advances in transportation. Not only were people, places, and events close to home recorded, but the camera became a natural companion to the world traveler.

As early as October 1839 photographers set out for the Middle East, where they made daguerreotypes, unique single images that could not be reproduced. Engravings copied from these photographs taken around the world appeared in N. P. Lerebours's *Excursions daguérriennes: Vues et monuments les plus remarquables du globe* (1840–1844). The calotype process, which allowed multiple prints to be produced from a paper negative, opened the possibility for photographically illustrated books such as Maxime Du Camp's *Egypte, Nubie, Palestine et Syrie* (1852). Although costly, this travel book proved to be a commercial success.

Technical innovations rapidly followed, making photography a somewhat less complicated science and more accessible to professionals and amateurs. Photographers under the auspices of commercial studios or scientific expeditions spread out over the globe—John Thompson in China, Bourne and Shepherd in India, the Bonfils family studio in the Near East, William H. Jackson and Timothy O'Sullivan in the United States western territories, Marc Ferrez in South America, Désiré Charnay in Central America. These pioneers mastered a fledgling technology and produced a magnificent record of the nineteenth-century world.

The camera arrived in Japan at a time when political unrest, a failing government, and foreign pressures to open the country to the West set the stage for sweeping changes that were to affect the course of subsequent Japanese history and culture. The opening of Japan in the early 1850s was followed by the establishment of treaty ports for foreigners. As the technology became more widely accepted, commercial and amateur photography by the 1860s began to flourish in these ports, where Americans, Europeans, and Japanese operated studios. By the turn of the century Japan had evolved from an insular country to an industrialized power. Ironically, Americans and Europeans introduced the technology of photography to record the traditions that were vanishing as a result of Western influence (plate 3).

Eliphalet Brown, Jr., of Philadelphia was the official photographer of Commodore Matthew C. Perry's mission to Japan in 1854, and his daguerreotypes were copied by lithographers to illustrate official reports of the expedition. In the 1860s, J. G. Gower, an English diplomatic aide and photographer, published *Views of Japan*. Beginning in the early 1860s, Felice Beato, a naturalized English subject born in Venice, operated a studio in Yokohama. He established a standard and approach that influenced the work of photographers who followed him. Rather than conveying a purely Westernized conception of Japanese culture, Beato's thoughtful compositions reflect his appreciation for the Japanese aesthetic. In 1877 Beato's studio was bought out by Baron Raimund Stillfried von Rathenitz, an Austrian nobleman, who expressed himself primarily through elegant and simply composed portraits.

Early on, the Japanese learned the art of photography from Westerners. Beato and Stillfried trained a generation of Japanese assistants who became first-rate photographers. However, the talents of the Japa-

Melissa Banta is Director of Photographic Archives at the Peabody Museum of Archaeology and Ethnology.

nese may have been generally underestimated as an 1884 article based on an interview with Stillfried suggests:

> Stillfried makes very interesting observations as to the position of photography in Eastern countries and says that the first photographer settled in Siam about 1857. He was a missionary, and he first converted a native to Christianity, and then taught him photography. This convert is still in Siam, and is neither a good Christian nor a high class photographer; still he turns out his work at so low a price that no European can compete with him.
>
> . . . nine tenths of the Japanese photographers [have] been, at one time or another, assistants to Baron von Stillfried. As soon as one of these assistants imagined himself to have learned enough to work independently, he ordinarily left, and established himself on his own account. When, however, these newly established photographers found that they could not make good pictures, they concluded that there was some mystery in regard to the preparations used, and in several cases it has happened that when a European photographer has been working in the streets, large sums have been offered for his working appliances taken as a whole.[1]

Stillfried's studio was taken over in 1885 by one of his apprentices, Kusakabe Kimbei, who also worked in portraiture. In 1886 A. Farsari acquired Stillfried's stock and went on to operate one of Japan's largest commercial photographic firms.

Commercial photography in Japan was the result of a unique cross-cultural exchange, which set it apart from other nineteenth-century travel and expeditionary photography, as demonstrated in the essays that follow. The medium offered a means of expression through which Westerners and Japanese mutually conveyed their vision of the newly opened country. This expression grew out of the technological options available to photographers, existing Western and Japanese artistic traditions they employed, and the social and cultural interaction among photographers, their subjects, and the audiences they served.

Nineteenth-century photographers overcame the challenge of a bulky camera, fragile glass-plate nega-

tives, long exposure times, and difficult processing procedures. They relied not only on established Western pictorial and photographic conventions but also found inspiration in Japanese artistic traditions such as the hand-colored wood-block print. This is evident in the kind of compositions commercial photographers favored and the practice of having their prints hand-colored by Japanese artisans. Not all depictions of the Japanese display the same sensitivity to composition and subject. In some anthropological photog-

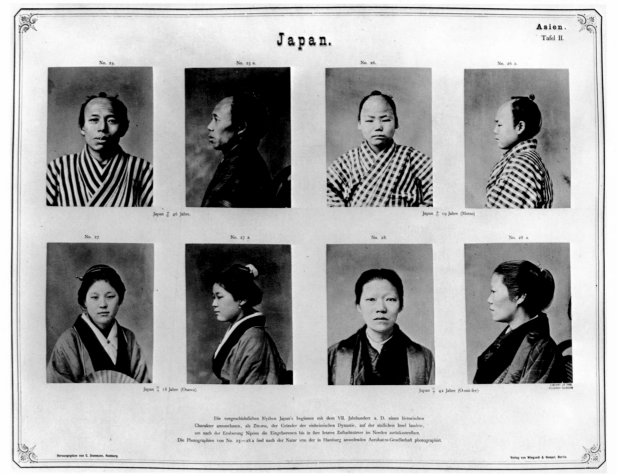

4. Photographer unknown, 1874
Albumen print (Courtesy Tozzer Library, Harvard University) *Anthropologisch-Ethnologisches Album in Photographien*

The aesthetic sensitivity found in commercial photography in nineteenth-century Japan distinguished it from the kind of anthropological photography that focused on physical and racial characteristics. These images were produced for the Berlin Society of Anthropology, Ethnology, and Prehistory and formed part of an album illustrating racial types from around the world.

raphy, the purpose of which was to provide visual evidence of physical and biological types, subjects were commonly reduced to front and side views typical of natural history specimens (plate 4).

Although some nineteenth-century images in Japan depict emerging cultural and technological innovations, on the whole commercial photography did not accurately represent the rapid modernization that took place. Instead, contemporary photographers sensed the need to capture disappearing traditions in the face of internal and external transformation. They thereby reinforced the oriental "mystique" in the West, where photography of foreign lands and peoples had become a popular commodity. Commercial images portrayed a wide spectrum of Japanese life including native "types," occupations, daily activities, and landscapes, as well as unusual and exotic subjects. The same process of inventorying cultural types occurred on the part of the Japanese as well: through wood-block prints they catalogued the diversity of foreign people arriving on their shores (plate 5).

While in Japan the photographic record may not have been a true testament to a rapidly changing society, beneath the attempt to accurately document a vanishing way of life lies a curiosity and respect not always evident in photographic renderings of other societies in the same period. Elsewhere, to satiate the tastes of a nineteenth-century tourist market, commercial photographers might pose subjects or professional models in studio costumes against painted backdrops which sometimes bore little relation to the culture it was intended to document (plate 6). In Japan, photographers focused on visually preserving traditional, albeit disappearing, ways of life (plate 7).

5. Issen Yoshikazu, 1861
Wood-block print (Courtesy Philadelphia Museum of Art)

A Russian couple holding a Yokohama print

Through the medium of wood-block prints, the Japanese compiled their own inventory of foreign cultural types.

6. Photographer unknown, ca. 1898
Albumen print (PM H31113)

Studio portrait of a tattooed man, Marquesas Islands, Polynesia.

Nineteenth-century photographic documentation took on a variety of forms, depending on the photographer's assumptions, purposes, and relationship to his subjects. In this picture, an incongruous backdrop distorts the realities of the culture presented.

7. Stillfried & Andersen Co. studio imprint, ca. 1860s–1870s
Albumen print (PM H15038)

A young man in the formal dress of a high-ranking samurai.

Commercial photographers in Japan were particularly sensitive to the cultural identity of the subjects they photographed.

The Collectors

Linked to the Peabody and Wellesley photographs is the story of their collectors, who were among the early members of Boston's elite cultural and academic circles traveling in Japan. The Japanese were immersed in absorbing Western ideas and technology, creating a climate favorable for Western travelers who sought to record and collect the traditions and antiquities of the country still unaltered by Western influence. Their endeavors had profound consequences for the cultural enrichment of those back home.

The Peabody Museum's photographs were donated on behalf of William Sturgis Bigelow. The circuitous origins of the collection can be traced to the travels of Edward Sylvester Morse. A self-educated zoologist, Morse worked with Louis Agassiz, a natural historian and founder of Harvard's Museum of Comparative Zoology. Morse established himself in Salem, Massachusetts, when George Peabody, founder of Harvard's Peabody Museum, gave support for expansion of Salem's East Indian Marine Society. It was renamed the Peabody Academy of Sciences, and in 1880 Morse began his 36-year tenure as its director.

Morse's 1877 trip to Japan in search of brachiopods (a class of mollusk) led to an invitation from the Imperial University of Tokyo to found a museum and organize a department of natural history.[2] Upon his return to New England two years later, Morse's series of lectures kindled interest in traditional Japanese culture among many Bostonians, including Percival Lowell, Henry Adams, John LaFarge, Isabella Stewart Gardner, and William Sturgis

8. Photographer unknown, 1885
Albumen print (Courtesy Benjamin LaFarge)
William Sturgis Bigelow dressed in Japanese hat and robe at Homyoin Temple, Kyoto.

Bigelow was a pioneer in fostering Western appreciation of oriental culture and antiquities. He traveled in Japan for seven years, and his gift of over 26,000 artifacts to the Boston Museum of Fine Arts formed the basis for their renowned Japanese and Chinese collections.

Bigelow, all of whom would make expeditions to Japan.

Dedication to art and public service came naturally to Bigelow. His father, Henry Jacob Bigelow, was a founder and trustee of the Boston Museum of Fine Arts. William Sturgis Bigelow graduated from Harvard Medical School in 1874 and continued his studies abroad for five years. He practiced medicine at Massachusetts General Hospital and was an instructor of surgery at Harvard Medical School. A few years later, Bigelow's commitment to the profession began to wane; his imagination was captured by Morse's travels.[3] A month spent together at Bigelow's summer home on Tuckernuck Island off Nantucket cultivated an exchange of ideas and a lifelong friendship. In May 1882 Bigelow and Morse left for Japan accompanied by Ernest Fenollosa, a colleague of Morse from Salem and professor of philosophy at the Imperial University, and Okakura Kakuzo, Fenollosa's former student.

They arrived at an auspicious moment for foreign collectors, albeit a vulnerable one for the Japanese. Modernization hit the country with an intensity and speed that temporarily blinded the Japanese to the value of their antiquities. Fascinated by Western civilization and ideals, the Japanese easily relinquished their treasures at undervalued prices. Before a Western market for Japanese artifacts emerged, Bigelow and his colleagues seized the opportunity to amass what would become the largest collection of Japanese art outside Asia. Through Morse, they gained official access to remote areas of the country, where, as Morse wrote:

> We shall see a little of the life of old Japan. Dr. Bigelow will secure many forms of swords, guards and lacquers, and Mr. Fenollosa will increase his remarkable collections of pictures, so that we shall have in the vicinity of Boston by far the greatest collection of Japanese art in the world.[4]

Morse was not unaware of the consequences of their good fortune: "the lifeblood of Japan is seeping from a hidden wound. They do not know how sad it is to let their beautiful treasures leave the country."[5] Bigelow, Morse, and Fenollosa had already gathered close to 9,000 objects, including paintings, prints, ceramics, swords, masks, and costumes. Morse expressed his concern to Okakura Kakuzo who spoke with officials in Tokyo. In 1884 Japan passed the Law of Kokuhō (National Treasures), decreeing the registration and restriction from export of remaining antiquities.

Bigelow continued collecting in Japan for seven years. His gift of over 26,000 artifacts to the Boston Museum of Fine Arts formed the basis of its renowned Japanese and Chinese collections. Such generosity accounted in part for the museum's addition at Copley Square, and, later, its permanent move to Huntington Avenue. Bigelow casually alluded to the need for expansion early on in an 1883 letter from Tokyo: "You will have to build a new wing on to the Museum when I get home this time. The present building will not begin to hold my accumulations."[6]

Bigelow cultivated a keen interest in many art forms and cultures, donating ethnographic and archaeological material from around the world to several institutions, including Harvard's Peabody Museum. He celebrated his love of Japanese traditions through numerous endeavors. In Japan he immersed himself in the study of Buddhism, participating in a priest's course of study and becoming a member of the Tendai sect. His Ingersoll Lecture, *Buddhism and Immortality*, presented originally at Harvard, is one of his few published writings; he tended to work behind the scenes avidly encouraging others like Morse and Fenollosa to publish their research.

Elected to the board of trustees of the Boston Museum of Fine Arts in 1891, Bigelow remained active in the affairs of the museum and the acquisition of new collections until his death in 1926. The Japanese government, recognizing that Bigelow's collection enhanced cross-cultural understanding, decorated him with the Order of the Rising Sun with rank of Commander. Upon his death, Bigelow requested that half his ashes be buried in Mt. Auburn Cemetery in Cambridge, Massachusetts, and the other half in a Buddhist temple in Japan next to Fenollosa's ashes.

Another member of Boston's elite to travel to Japan in the late 1880s was Mary Alice Knox, instructor of history at Wellesley College. In 1886, she left on a world tour to spend the year in Japan, China, and India, gathering material with which to open a course on oriental history for the coming year. Prior to her trip, Miss Knox's classes had been limited to the history of European civilization. In the same year Mary's brother, the Reverend George William Knox, was appointed professor of philosophy and ethics at the Imperial University of Tokyo, a position he held until his return to America in 1893. Although no direct evidence indicates they traveled together, it is quite likely the Reverend Knox accompanied his sister through Japan and assisted her in research on Japanese customs and culture. Undoubtedly his familiarity with Japan influenced her decision to make such a trip.

George Knox maintained an interest in Japan throughout his distinguished teaching career. He was a professor of philosophy and history of religion at Union Theological Seminary, New York, and the Nathaniel Taylor Lecturer at Yale in 1903, and lectured extensively in India, China, and Japan from 1911 to 1912. He authored several books on Japanese culture and religion including *Autobiography of Arai-Hakuseki* (1902); *Japanese Life in Town and Country* (1905); and *The Development of Religion in Japan* (1907).

Wellesley's contact with Japan extended beyond curriculum-related affairs. In 1876 Henry Fowle Durant, founder of Wellesley College, sent a portfolio of information on the college to the Japanese Department of Education; in 1888 Wellesley hosted its first foreign student, a Japanese woman named Kin Kato.

The Bigelow and Knox collections include 95 and 134 photographs respectively, comprising the largest components of the institutions' photographs of Japan. The collectors' selections, which overlap in only one print, invite comparison. Bigelow had a penchant for alluring exotic portrayals of women. The few photographs of women that Mary Knox chose show them engaged in the activities of wife or mother. Bigelow's group is primarily composed of expressive portraits, including men of social rank and theatrical performers. Mary Knox's prints reveal her affinity for beautifully composed landscape and architectural scenes, including monuments and historic temples (all noticeably absent from the Bigelow prints). Both groups include representations of daily life and customs, reflecting the collectors' shared interest in providing a broad view of Japanese life and culture.

Westerners in Japan witnessed the transformation of Japanese society within a compressed time period. As Morse wrote:

Japan had within a few years emerged from a peculiar state of civilization which had endured for centuries. . . . changes had taken place, such as the modern training of its armies; a widespread system of public schools, government departments of war, treasury, agriculture, telegraph, post, statistics, and other bureaus of modern administration,—all these instrumentalities making a slight impress on the large cities such as Tokyo and Osaka, sufficiently marked however to cause one to envy those who only a few years before had seen the people when all the samurai wore the two swords, when every man wore the queue and every married woman blackened the teeth.[7]

Bigelow and Knox, like the commercial photographers whose prints they collected, chose to preserve Japanese tradition by fostering Western appreciation of it. Bigelow expressed the urgency of this mission to Morse:

You are still frittering away your valuable time on the lower forms of animal life, which anybody can attend to, instead of devoting it to the highest, about the manners and customs of which no one is so well qualified to speak as you. . . . Drop your damned Brachiopods. . . . Remember that the Japanese organisms which you and I knew familiarly are vanishing types, many of which have

Miss Knox is warmly welcomed after her tour around the world accomplished without accident or serious sickness. She has opened her new course in the "History of Oriental Civilization" which promises to be one of much interest. She is prepared to present the subject by the modern laboratory method with numerous illustrations.
Wellesley Courant, September 29, 1887

9. McCormick, 1885
Albumen print (Courtesy Wellesley College Archives)
Mary Alice Knox.

An instructor of history at Wellesley College, Knox made a world tour from 1886 to 1887. The photographs she collected in Japan were used in her courses on oriental civilization at the college, offered for the first time upon her return.

already disappeared completely from the face of the earth, and that men of our age are literally the last people who have seen these organisms alive.[8]

The Interpreters

The impact of photography was revolutionary in its potential to record "reality" and to widely disseminate information. The new technology brought forth an entirely new way of seeing. Marketed by the mil-

lions, photographs fed a public eager for convincing visual renderings of exotic worlds.[9]

In Yokohama, foreign newspapers carried notices from Japanese photographers advertising both their services and copious supplies of images (plate 10). A Russian visitor at the turn of the century observed the ever-increasing interest in this popular commodity:

Yokohama is the most convenient place to buy Japanese photographs. The photographers such as Ogawa, Suzuki, Kimbei, and Tamamura can hardly fill the de-

10. *The Japanese Herald*, September 20, 1862
(Courtesy Yokohama Archives of History)
Photographers' services were well advertised in foreign newspapers in Japan.

11. Photographer unknown, ca. 1860–1868
Albumen print mounted on stereocard (PM H15343 and PM H15344)

Japanese diplomatic mission sent to the West.

Nineteenth-century photographs were reproduced in a variety of formats including stereographs, a popular form of entertainment from the 1850s on. When viewed through a stereoscope, two images merge to appear as a single, three-dimensional image. This photograph may have been taken by the Charles D. Fredericks studio, as it shows the same backdrop and props found in Fredericks's other images of Japanese diplomats.

mand of the foreigners who arrive from abroad by ship. Their usual practice is to take the photographs and later on pack them in tin boxes and send them to the orderers.[10]

Images were produced as single prints or in immensely popular formats such as stereocards, cartes-de-visite, and cabinet cards bought individually or bound in albums (plate 11). Once exported to Western countries, they would be advertised and distributed through photographic shops and traveling salesmen. By 1875 the development of several photomechanical printing processes made possible the incorporation of photographic images within book texts. George Knox, for example, used prints of several photographs found in the Peabody and Wellesley collections to illustrate his book *Japanese Life in Town and Country.*

Photographs were also reproduced or copied in the form of glass lantern slides, which were then projected with a device known as the magic lantern (plate 12). The import of this new medium alone was profound:

This instrument is now fast taking its deserved position as the medium pre-eminent for the diffusion of knowledge, and for the instruction and amusement of persons of all ages, and all classes of society. This has been brought about, in a great measure, by the important improvements which have taken place both in the lanterns and in the pictures used as illustrations, as well as by the growing desire for scientific knowledge which seems to characterize this generation.[11]

The spread of colonial empires and technological advances of the nineteenth century ushered in a new era of inquiry typified by the disciplines of natural science and anthropology. Government officials, scientists, scholars, and travelers set out to study and understand their relationship to alien cultures. Commercial photography thus served many purposes and audiences. For Western travelers to Japan, photographic prints provided a visual souvenir of their journeys. For others, the images offered a first glimpse of unfamiliar cultures, igniting their imagination and curiosity. Accompanied by little or no documentation, the photograph sometimes represented the only visual opportunity by which to observe another culture.

Educational institutions acquired photographic documentation for research and teaching. Upon Mary Alice Knox's return from her world tour in 1887, she began teaching the first course offered at

[18]

虹燈寫心競

洋行

暢游開延華

12. Chikanobu Yoshu, 1890
Wood-block print (© Mondadori-Shueisha)

Traveling Abroad

Photographs of foreign peoples and places were further enforced in the public mind through the invention of an instrument known as the magic lantern, which projected glass slides. The device was popular in Japan as well as the West; here a Japanese woman illustrates her trip abroad.

Wellesley on oriental civilization, attended that year by nineteen students.

> Miss Knox is warmly welcomed after her tour around the world, accomplished without accident or serious sickness. She has opened her new course in the "History of Oriental Civilization" which promises to be one of much interest. She has prepared to present the subject by the modern laboratory method with numerous illustrations.[12]

That these "illustrations" would have included the photographs she brought from Japan and donated to Wellesley would not be surprising. Mary Knox's acquisition of photographs of Japan as well as several photographs of India was indicated in a catalogue entry in the first volume documenting photograph accessions to the art department. Used for illustration and educational purposes, they naturally became the property of the art department located, at the time, in Wellesley College Hall with the other academic disciplines. It was usual practice for photographs, reproductions, and plaster casts to be placed in College Hall for study by students.

Bigelow's niece, Mary Lothrop, donated her uncle's photographs to Harvard's Peabody Museum shortly after his death in 1926. In this ethnological institution their significance lay in the depiction of customs, religion, art, and social and political systems; they enhanced the researcher's attempt to gather and interpret cultural data. The context in which an image is placed can acutely alter the meaning one might elicit from it. The Peabody photographs of the Japanese embassy in the United States present a case in point (plate 13). The camera was there to record the historic arrival of these diplomatic missions

sent to the West in the 1860s. Louis Agassiz, who originally collected the prints for Harvard's Museum of Comparative Zoology, found in them another significance. Like many other photographs of human subjects he collected, they provided visual data for his analysis of racial types.

In Western countries today institutions are reawakening to the value of their archival photographs and have rediscovered fine collections of nineteenth-century prints. In Japan, where most commercial photographs were exported for the tourist trade, a new interest in these collections has arisen. The interpretive process continues, and the photograph takes on new life. "A Timely Encounter" celebrates these images from Eastern and Western perspectives, examining the cultural, technological, and artistic contexts in which they were created and used. By exploring the visual language conveyed through the photograph, we deepen our understanding of one culture's interpretation of the other.

13. Charles D. Fredericks, 1860–1868
Salt print (PM H15322)

Japanese delegate in New York.

The Japanese missions sent to the West were photographed in fashionable studios. Louis Agassiz, founder of Harvard's Museum of Comparative Zoology, collected photographs like these not for their historical significance, but as visual data for his analysis of racial types.

NOTES

1. "Photography in Eastern Asia," *The Photographic News* 28(1330):129.
2. One of Morse's important contributions was the discovery of the Ōmori shellmound outside of Tokyo.
3. Arthur Fairbanks, *William Sturgis Bigelow 1850–1926*, p. 508. Fairbanks states that Bigelow "gifted as he was in keenness of mind and deftness of hand, was unfitted by temperament for active practice."
4. Van Wyck Brooks, *Fenollosa and His Circle*, p. 27.
5. Walter Muir Whitehill, *Museum of Fine Arts, Boston: A Centennial History*, Vol. 1, p. 109.
6. Bigelow to General Loring, May 26, 1883, Boston Museum of Fine Arts Archives, Boston, Mass.
7. Edward S. Morse, *Japan Day By Day*, Vol. 1, p. ix.
8. Ibid., pp. ix–x.
9. Beaumont Newhall, *The History of Photography*, pp. 85–116.
10. Daiichi Art Center, ed., "Shashin no makuake," Vol. 1, p. 154.
11. William Welling, *Photography in America: The Formative Years 1839–1900*, p. 237.
12. *Wellesley Courant*, September 29, 1887. Wellesley, Mass.

BIBLIOGRAPHY

Barthes, Roland
1981 *Camera Lucida: Reflections on Photography.* New York: Hill and Wang.

Bigelow, William Sturgis
1908 *Buddhism and Immortality.* The Ingersoll Lecture. Boston and New York: Houghton Mifflin Co.

Brooks, Van Wyck
1962 *Fenollosa and his Circle.* New York: E. P. Dutton and Co., Inc.

Daiichi Art Center, ed.
1985 *Shashin no makuake.* Vol. 1 of *Nihon shashin zenshū.* Shōgakukan.

Du Camp, Maxime
1852 *Egypte, Nubie, Palestine et Syrie.* Paris.

Fairbanks, Arthur
n.d. "William Sturgis Bigelow 1850–1926." *Proceedings of the American Academy.*

Fields, Rick
1981 *How the Swans Came to the Lake: A Narrative History of Buddhism in America.* Boulder: Shambhala Publications Inc.

Ford, Worthington Chauncey
1938 *Letters of Henry Adams.* Boston and New York: Houghton Mifflin Co.

Gower, J. G.
1861 *Views of Japan.* London: Negretti and Zambra.

Japan Photographers Association
1980 *A Century of Japanese Photography.* Introduction by John W. Dower. New York: Pantheon Books, Random House.

Knox, George William
1902 *Autobiography of Arai-Hakuseki.* Asiatic Society of Japan.
1905 *Japanese Life in Town and Country.* New York and London: G. P. Putnam's Sons.
1907 *The Development of Religion in Japan.* New York and London: G. P. Putnam's Sons.
1908 *The Direct and Fundamental Proofs of the Christian Religion.* New York: Charles Scribner's Sons.

Lerebours, N. P.
1842 *Excursions daguérriennes: Vues et monuments les plus remarquables du globe.* Paris: Rittner et Goupil.

Morse, Edward S.
1917 *Japan Day by Day 1877, 1878–79, 1882–83.* Vols. 1 and 2. Boston and New York: Houghton Mifflin Co.

Newhall, Beaumont
1982 *The History of Photography.* New York: Museum of Modern Art.

Photographic News
1884 "Photography in Eastern Asia." *The Photographic News* 28 (1330):129. London: Piper and Carter.

Taft, Robert
1938 *Photography and the American Scene: A Social History, 1839–1889.* New York: Dover.

Vaczek, Louis, and Gail Buckland
1981 *The Travelers in Ancient Lands: A Portrait of the Middle East, 1839–1919.* Boston: New York Graphic Society.

Wellesley Courant
1887 *Wellesley Courant* (September 29, 1887). Wellesley, Massachusetts.

Welling, William
1978 *Photography in America: The Formative Years 1839–1900.* New York: Thomas Y. Crowell Co.

Whitehill, Walter Muir
1977 *Museum of Fine Arts, Boston: A Centennial History.* Vols. 1 and 2. Cambridge, Massachusetts. Harvard University Press.

Wirgman, Charles
1885 *A Sketchbook of Japan.* Yokohama: R. Meiklejohn and Co.

Worswick, Clark
1979 *Japan: Photographs 1854–1905.* Introduction by Jan Morris and A. Pennwick. New York: Alfred A. Knopf.

14. Cultural and urban centers of nineteenth-century Japan. (Courtesy Barbara Isaac)

The photographs in this exhibition were taken by commercial photographers whose activities around the time of the Meiji Restoration were mainly limited to treaty ports like Yokohama and surrounding areas. Yokohama was not representative of the more traditional cultural or political urban centers such as those of Edo (Tokyo) or Kyoto.

N

Edo (Tokyo)

Yokohama

Kyoto •

Nagasaki

Western Images, Japanese Identities: Cultural Dialogue between East and West in Yokohama Photography

HARUKO IWASAKI

The early photographs of Japan in the Bigelow and Knox collections hold multiple attractions for today's audience. The most immediate appeal is aesthetic—the sheer beauty of the people and landscapes so finely captured by Felice Beato, Baron Raimund Stillfried von Rathenitz and other Western photographers of the nineteenth century. Nostalgia is undoubtedly a further appeal. Glimpses of the unspoiled mountains and lakes of pre-industrial Japan readily stir in us a poignant longing when contrasted with the steel-and-glass images of today's Japan. The documentary value of the collection is also evident. Seemingly frozen in time, the long-vanished customs and manners of feudal Japan appear safely preserved here, to instruct and intrigue.

But if we probe more deeply, we can see that these photographs also tell a story, that of the complex and ambivalent dialogue between Japan and the West in the second half of the nineteenth century. The connotations of these images for Western viewers is only half the story; it is necessary to understand how they fit into the Japanese context as well. This essay attempts to present the emergence of photography within the changing social and cultural context of Japan both before and after the Meiji Restoration of 1868. Only by understanding the relationship between Western and Japanese photographers and the relationship between the images and the realities they sought to capture can we make sense of them.

The Bigelow and Knox collections of photographs reflect a time of unprecedented upheaval and change in the history of Japan, during which the self-contained, feudal land was transformed into an assertive modern state, able to compete on equal footing with the Western imperialist powers. These years are divided by the Meiji Restoration of 1868 into the "Bakumatsu"—literally, "the end of the Bakufu [Tokugawa shogun's government, 1853–1868]"—and the early Meiji periods. The Restoration brought an end to two and a half centuries of feudal rule by the Tokugawa Shogunate and began the modern Meiji state, which was governed in form by the newly restored imperial house. It was in the Bakumatsu period that photography began to spread in Japan, and that Felice Beato started his thriving studio in Yokohama. Then, in the early Meiji period, came the rapid development of a market for photographs of Japan that could be sold to visiting Western tourists. It was at the height of the rapid changes of Meiji, in the 1880s, that William Sturgis Bigelow and Mary Alice Knox purchased their photographs. Because the political and cultural climates of these two periods are very different, and hence result in different interpretations of their respective photographic images, it is best to treat them separately.

Bakumatsu Period

The Bakumatsu period spans the years from the arrival of Commodore Matthew C. Perry in 1853 until the collapse of the Bakufu in 1868, years of violence and chaos. During this period, the Bakufu in Edo (Tokyo), the Imperial court in Kyoto, and the powerful feudal lords in the provinces wrestled both diplomatically and, in the end, militarily for national hegemony. Heavy pressures from abroad meanwhile compelled the Bakufu to accept a series of unequal treaties with foreigners, to send seven diplomatic missions to the West from 1860 to 1868 and to open the three ports of Nagasaki, Yokohama, and Hakodate in 1859 to foreign diplomats and traders. These desperate measures by the Bakufu triggered an extreme range of responses. They outraged the xenophobic factions and drove some to violence against foreigners. But the West's swift and effective reprisals convinced the better-informed of the feudal lords, Bakufu officials, and scholars of an acute need to learn from the West.

The first surge of interest in photography in pre-Restoration Japan was a part of this Westernizing movement among the enlightened factions of the ruling class. Despite the general fear of the West, a number of influential lords, above all Shimazu Nariakira of Satsuma, mobilized their resources and directed scholars of Rangaku (Western studies) to gain a knowledge of photography.[1] Some of these samurai initiates learned the rudiments of the art in Nagasaki from Dutch physician Pompe van Meedervoort and French photographer Rossier, among others.[2] The Nagasaki group included Ueno Hikoma, whose merchant father Shunnojō had procured for Lord Shimazu the first daguerreotype camera to enter Japan. Those in eastern Japan went to Yokohama to try to absorb the technique from the growing foreign population there. These early Japanese students of photography in Yokohama included the well-known Rangaku scholar Sakuma Shōzan and an enterprising commoner by the name of Shimooka Renjō, a student of the Kanō school of painting.

Haruko Iwasaki is Assistant Professor of Japanese in the Department of East Asian Languages and Civilizations at Harvard University.

The keen interest in photography initiated by the ruling class was further whetted in the 1860s by the Bakufu diplomatic missions to the West. Whether in San Francisco, New York, Paris, or Berlin, many of the delegates eagerly had their portraits taken and brought them home with them (plate 13). The first mission to Europe (1862) included Lord Shimazu's subject, Matsuki Kōan, who had translated Dutch documents on photography and had been instructed in the art by Rossier. On his visit to the celebrated Nadar portrait studio in Paris, the enthralled Matsuki Kōan left a note in Japanese, "Photography is the Creator's painting; and its luminosity, His brush."[3] Two years later, in 1864, the members of the second mission to Europe had a memorable portrait taken on their stop-over in Egypt, a startling image of about two dozen sworded samurai gathered below the Sphinx in profile. It bears the signature "A. Beato"—now known to be the brother of the famous photojournalist Felice, who was already operating in Japan.[4]

Yokohama Photography

It was in this turbulent Bakumatsu era, mainly within the confines of the Yokohama foreign settlement, that Felice Beato and other artists laid the basis for the commercial photography represented in the Bigelow and Knox collections. As noted elsewhere, American daguerreotypist Eliphalet Brown, Jr., had already accompanied Perry's mission and extensively recorded Japan, although unfortunately almost none of his works survives. The report of the expedition and the eventual opening of the country to foreign travel created waves of curiosity in the West, turning Japan into a prime target for global journalism. Artists and photographers were among the first of the motley group of adventurers from the West who began to arrive in Yokohama soon after this fishing village was opened in 1859. Felice Beato is believed to have ar-

rived by the summer of 1863, probably at the urging of his artist friend Charles Wirgman, who had reached Japan in 1861.[5] Beato first operated in partnership with Wirgman, then opened his own studio at No. 17 on the Bund.

Beato's colorful trail tells us much about life in Yokohama as well as about the man himself.[6] Jovial and gregarious, the Venetian-born cosmopolitan attracted many Western and Japanese friends and enjoyed bowling, riding, and the other amusements of the settlement. Beato's escapades were often reported by Wirgman in the *Japan Punch*, where he was referred to as "Count Collodion." One such incident was "The Great Rolled Beef Case" of October 11, 1875, in which Beato became enraged when his Japanese cook served him a kind of steak he disliked disguised as "rolled beef." Infuriated, the photographer hurled the plate at the cook and injured him, resulting in a suit and a fine of one dollar plus doctor's costs (plate 15). The professional career of the talented and restless Beato was just as colorful. He not only prospered as a photographer but, in his two decades in Japan, he also made—and eventually lost—a fortune in the export-import business, real estate, and speculation in the rice and silver markets.

The boom town of Yokohama attracted many speculative Japanese as well, who sought lucrative business with the foreigners. One such migrant was the self-made photographer Shimooka Renjō, who presents an interesting comparison with a Western adventurer like Beato. Working outside the samurai establishment, the impoverished former artist gathered scraps of information on photography and, after years of struggle, finally succeeded in producing salable prints. The studio he opened in Yokohama in 1862, together with that of Ueno Hikoma in Nagasaki in the same year, was the first in Japan. After initial success as a photographer, however, Shimooka Renjō—like Beato—moved on to other enterprises, including a Tokyo-Yokohama carriage service, gas lighting, and a milk business. He abandoned

15. Charles Wirgman
Japan Punch, December, 1875 (Courtesy Widener Library, Harvard University)

The Great Rolled Beef Case

Photographer Felice Beato was a colorful public figure whose escapades were often reported in *Japan Punch*, an illustrated newspaper for foreigners. This cartoon depicts a well-known incident between Beato and his Japanese cook, and the ensuing court case.

one such endeavor after another, however, and eventually died destitute.[7] It was of such colorful characters that the early history of Yokohama photography is composed.

To understand Yokohama photography, two factors require our attention. One is the xenophobic climate of the Bakumatsu period when Beato was most active. During the violent years of the mid-1860s, Beato had often risked his life on photographic expeditions and now was obliged for the most part to remain in his Yokohama studio, relying on the limited kind of sitters available in the foreign settlement. Hurriedly established in a bleak fishing village twenty-five miles from Edo, Yokohama had little of the traditional culture to offer. Violence against Westerners did end with the Restoration of 1868, but xenophobic sentiment persisted for decades in more covert form, limiting Westerners' full contact with Japanese society.

Tourism was another, and increasingly influential, factor for Yokohama photographers. Western and Japanese photographers alike found their prime clientele among the Western visitors. Beato did continue to do some journalistic photography, and Stillfried worked for the Japanese government for short periods in the 1870s, but their steady customers were those who kept landing at the wharf. The same was true with the Japanese photographers, who found little business among their countrymen at the time. One problem for the Japanese was the prohibitive cost. A portrait photograph usually cost half a *ryō* (gold piece) per head, equal to the monthly pay of an artisan.[8] Even more important, perhaps, was the Japanese fear of photography, still widespread among the commoners in the 1860s. Entrepreneurs such as Shimooka Renjō were able to survive these lean years mainly through sales to tourists.

Yokohama photography thus came to appeal first and foremost to tourist tastes. Predictably, the emphasis was on traditional Japan, the idyllic land of Mt. Fuji, serene lakes dotted with sails, proud two-sworded samurai, almond-eyed "geisha" in semi-nude poses, and decapitated heads on display at the execution grounds. Shimooka Renjō even simulated a scene of harakiri.[9] Over time, these photographs thus helped to establish the basic cluster of stereotyped images of Japan, the "Fujiyama-geisha" complex which survives strongly to the present day. Shimooka Renjō, who contributed to this trend as much as did the Western photographers, seems to have had some qualms later. In reminiscing on his prime years in photography, he reflected that his efforts to cater to the taste for exoticism of tourists may have contributed to a distorted image of Japan in the United States and Europe.[10]

This is not to say that the images in the Bigelow and Knox collections misrepresent nineteenth-century Japan. On the contrary, they contain few images that grossly distort the reality of the time. It would be more accurate to say that they are a generally faithful portrayal of certain areas of Japanese life at a specific time in its history. These areas of life were selected largely from what was available to foreign photographers based in Yokohama, with an eye to the market demands. The period extended through the Bakumatsu several years into the Meiji era. But the question of authenticity becomes a more complex issue by the time of Bigelow and Knox's purchases in the 1880s, because of the enormous change that had begun to take place in the intervening decade and a half.

Meiji Restoration

The first decades after the Meiji Restoration saw change of a scope virtually unequaled in the preceding history of the country. The young emperor moved from Kyoto to the new capital of Tokyo (Edo) and resumed the form of direct imperial rule. A series of structural reforms were rapidly implemented to transform the largely feudal state into a modern monarchy: feudal classes were effectively abolished, feudal domains replaced by prefectures, and efforts begun to formulate a constitution. A campaign was launched against feudal customs and manners. A decree issued in 1871 endorsed the removal of top knots and the cessation of sword-bearing. The emperor himself, dressed in ancient court costume, was photographed in 1872 by Uchida Kuichi, a disciple of Ueno Hikoma. A year later Uchida Kuichi had to take a completely new set of photographs to portray the emperor transformed, decked out in a new Western-style military uniform and with a fresh haircut (see plate 2). In 1872, the first railroad in a network of iron rails that would cover the country by the end of the century connected Tokyo and Yokohama. Telephone, telegraph, gaslight, postal service and other modern conveniences changed the lives of people, while sukiyaki (a new invention following the end of the customary ban on meat-eating) and beer began attracting Japanese, especially in Yokohama. By the late 1870s, over half of the boys were in school, youths marched in the new conscript army, and young women had begun to work at steam-driven textile mills.

When William Sturgis Bigelow landed at Yokohama in 1882, signs of change must have been everywhere. Mary Alice Knox must have seen the changes intensified, because her arrival around 1886 corresponds to the Rokumeikan (Deer-Cry Pavilion) period, when the drive for Westernization had reached its peak.[11] And yet the photographs they acquired reflect little of such changes. The images in Bigelow's collection seem to date back about a decade or more, to the 1860s or early 1870s, judging by the hair styles and clothing, as well as the serial numbers on the photographs. Those in the Wellesley collection seem to belong to later years, but they are predominantly of rural Japan, where visible change was almost nonexistent. The few contemporary details in urban scenes are those unwittingly included in the background, such as the flag advertising beef on a Yokohama street (plate 16). One exception is a photograph illustrating the transformation of a samurai, evocative of the popular caricatures of the Yokohama artist Georges Bigot: the image of a samurai in his formal costume is paired with the rather bizarre depiction of the same man, behatted and frozen in an ill-fitting frock coat (plates 17 and 18). In an era of rapid cultural change, the persistence of the older images created an increasing disparity with reality, ironically encouraging the impression that Japan was not changing at all, but rather locked into the set poses of an idyllic pre-industrial age. Such distortion is nonetheless understandable. The buyers of the Yokohama photographs were mostly there to discover the exquisite and exotic Orient—not to enjoy crude imitations of what they themselves had developed.

16. Studio unknown, ca. 1870s–1880s
Hand-colored albumen print (WCM 4614, Gift of Miss M. A. Hawley)

The theater district of Yokohama.

The shop sign on the right advertises the formerly forbidden delicacy, beef—a sign of change unwittingly captured within a nostalgic tourist picture.

Japan had within a few years emerged from a peculiar state of civilization which had endured for centuries. . . . changes had taken place, such as the modern training of its armies; a widespread system of public schools, government departments of war, treasury, agriculture, telegraph, post, statistics, and other bureaus of modern administration, all these instrumentalities making a slight impress on the larger cities such as Tokyo and Osaka, sufficiently marked however to cause one to envy those who only a few years before had seen the people when all the samurai wore the two swords, when every man wore the queue, and every married woman blackened the teeth.

EDWARD S. MORSE, 1877
Japan Day By Day

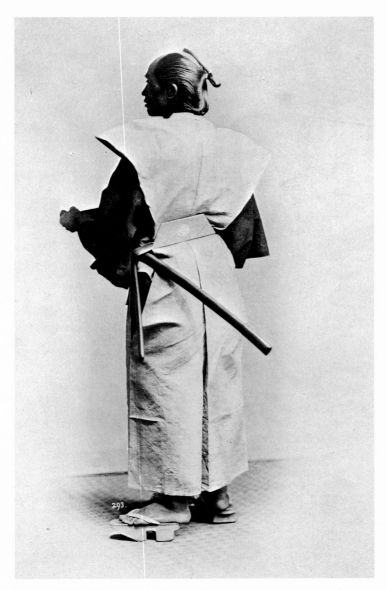

17, 18. Stillfried & Andersen Co. studio imprint, ca. 1860s–1870s

Albumen print (PM H15210 & PM H15211)

Transformation of samurai.

Cultural changes such as these were rarely documented in Japanese commercial photography of the period.

19. Studio unknown, ca. 1870s–1880s
Hand-colored albumen print (WCM a1358)
The view of Mt. Fuji viewed through the trees on the Tōkaidō highway was a standard subject in Japanese art, reinterpreted through the modern medium of photography.

LANDSCAPES

The landscape photographs in the exhibition suggest certain links with traditional Japanese art. The most evident connection is a commonality of the places depicted, which in photographs tended to be the same "famous scenic spots" that had become standardized in ukiyo-e landscape prints, whether the temples and gardens of Edo or scenes along the Tōkaidō highway. One finds a further similarity of composition, with the photographs adopting the same technique of a close-up element against a more distant scenic background. These close-up objects, often a tree or flowers, tended to serve as a kind of framing device for the image as a whole, as in numerous photographs of Fuji (plate 19).

These similarities to existing pictorial art are no coincidence, since a number of the Japanese who became early photographers had themselves begun as painters—such as Shimooka Renjō, who was trained in the Kanō school and learned his new craft directly from Westerners. Even without such personal contact, the Western photographers would have had ample opportunity to see and buy color wood-block prints, which were conspicuously displayed in bookstores. This kind of contact with the color print may also be a link to the widespread practice of hand-tinting the photographs that were sold to tourists. Beato, for example, had eight Japanese working for him in 1872, four as photographers and four as tinters, in addition to his assistant, H. Woolett.[12]

SOCIAL TYPES

The portraits of Japanese people in these collections reflect the structure of pre-modern Japanese society. Throughout its long feudal rule, the Tokugawa gov-

20. Stillfried & Andersen Co. studio imprint, ca. 1860s–1870s
Hand-colored albumen print (PM H15034)

Samurai standing in front of backdrop painted with the image of Mt. Fuji, a depiction reinforcing the stereotypical view of Japan.

ernment enforced various measures to preserve class distinctions, especially those dividing the samurai class from commoners. And even within classes (particularly the samurai), there were elaborate regulations designed to reflect and preserve status.

The faces we see in the photographs tend to reveal this highly differentiated society. The samurai on the whole tend to look alert; their eyes have a certain daring which would not be found in their counterparts today, the elite government bureaucrats. In a reflection of their class and training, the samurai in portraits refuse to be mere objects: their looks are powerful and focused, as though they were staring into the face of the challenge of the West (plate 20). In contrast, the faces of townsmen and peasants are generally impassive, in the pose of deference expected of them. The photographers were instrumental as well in bringing out these social distinctions through composition and the posing of their subjects.

OCCUPATIONS

The townsmen included here are those easily visible from the street and the most readily available to the photographer—entertainers, street vendors, and artisans. The sheer variety of these types evokes the shop fronts and streets described in many works of Edo popular literature and in the travel journals of foreigners. Streets were filled with performances of all sorts, creating a rich mix of sight and sound: blind masseurs blew piercing whistles, candymen jangled bells and sang strange ballads, child lion dancers performed acrobatics to the beating of drums, and lottery vendors cranked away at their wheels of fortune (plates 21 and 22).

21. Stillfried & Andersen Co. studio imprint, ca. 1860s–1870s
Hand-colored albumen print (PM H15032)

A blind masseur with a whistle to announce himself to customers.

22. Stillfried & Andersen Co. studio imprint, ca. 1860s–1870s
Albumen print (PM H15023)
Divination lottery (*Omikuji*), outside of shrine or temple, where individuals "bought" their fortune.

The wide variety of small merchants, vendors, and artisans was well documented, while the merchant magnates are conspicuously missing from these commercial photographs.

Conspicuously absent from the townsmen group is the wealthy townsmen class, who lived their lives in private, out of people's view. Although some of them had amassed riches comparable to those of the ruling lords and could well bear the expense of photography, they seem not to have been as eager customers as samurai. This seems to fit with the low profile they kept and the cautious distance they maintained from foreigners during the Bakumatsu period.

THEATER

Theatrical performers were another fascination for commercial photographers. They included three types. One is now an almost extinct group, the Bugaku dancers, who performed ancient dances adopted by the Japanese from the Asian mainland in the Nara period. The second group, the Nō theater, was of medieval origin and maintained its conservative tradition through the patronage of the samurai class in the Tokugawa period. The collections contain splendid photographs of Nō costumes and masks (plate 23). The third type of theater was Kabuki, central to the popular culture of the Tokugawa period. Actors are posed either assuming a dramatic stance or appearing in famous scenes reenacted in studio settings (plate 24).

WOMEN

A variety of female portraits can be found in the Wellesley and Peabody collections, including courtesans and genteel women (plate 25). The beauty and number of these images in Yokohama photographs demonstrate that Japanese women composed one of the main ingredients of the "lure of the Orient."

23. Studio unknown, ca. 1870s–1880s
Hand-colored albumen print (PM 15131)
A male Nō actor wearing a young woman's mask and costume.

24. Studio unknown, ca. 1870s–1880s
Hand-colored albumen print (PM H15198)

A Kabuki actor in a dramatic stance.

Theatrical performers were a standard subject for commercial photographers.

26. Stillfried & Andersen Co. studio imprint, ca. 1860s–1870s

Hand-colored albumen print (PM H14988)

A Japanese prostitute.

Nineteenth-century photographs in Japan presented a variety of women, including prostitutes willing to pose seminude.

25. Studio unknown, ca. 1870s–1880s

Hand-colored albumen print (WCM 4599, Gift of Miss M. A. Hawley)

A young woman practicing calligraphy.

In fact, the rhapsodical account of the female in Japan had spread to the West long before the Restoration. Ernest Satow, a member of the British mission to Bakumatsu Japan, reminisced in his *A Diplomat in Japan* about how Laurence Oliphant's glowing tales of Japan had affected him. Satow promptly gave up his position at Cambridge University and applied for the position of student interpreter. Such romanticized images of Japanese women were further reinforced by the works of Pierre Loti, who visited Japan in 1885 and 1900.

Adulation by the Western male seems to have been a lopsided phenomenon, however. In the Bakumatsu and early Meiji periods, the female company readily accessible to the Westerners was limited to prostitutes in the special quarters licensed for foreigners. In Yokohama, it was the Miozaki brothels, established by the Bakufu in 1862. This was not a show of Bakufu hospitality but a continuation of the traditional policy of containing, rather than suppressing, prostitution.

The women who drifted to Miozaki found themselves doubly doomed. They not only suffered the general degradation of women in prostitution but as those who catered to "Western barbarians," they constituted the lowest of the low in the highly differentiated hierarchy of the Japanese demimonde. Westerners' concubines were derisively called *rashamen* (Western sheep) and were the objects of much notoriety and contempt.[13] Popular literature of the time exploited the voyeuristic curiosity of the public about these women who consorted with foreigners. One illustrated book (*Yokohama Matsudaibanashi*) reports the "most unusual tale" of a baby born of a

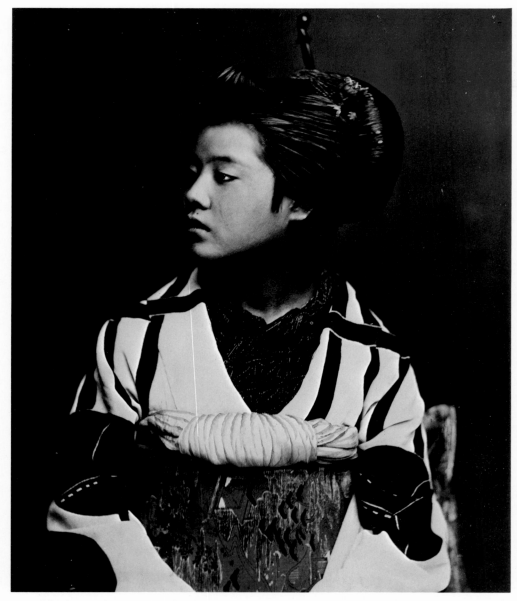

27. Stillfried & Andersen Co. studio imprint, ca. 1860s–1870s
Albumen print (PM H14984)
A prostitute, probably in her early teens.

foreigner and a Japanese woman, who came into the world "with a full set of teeth and thick beard." The illustration shows a hairy, tiny *gaijin* (foreigner) frolicking in the baby bath.[14]

Another story, widely circulated in the late 1850s, concerns a Miozaki woman named Kiyū, who was employed at the prosperous Gankirō house to entertain its Japanese clientele. As the story goes, an American resident of Yokohama fell in love with Kiyū and offered a large sum to the owner to procure her. When the owner pressed her, Kiyū retired to her room, lit some incense, and committed suicide. She left this poem:

> The courtesan—flower of Japan
> Bears scarcely a drop of dew.
> Never will she let her sleeves
> Be caught in American rain!

This episode of the 1860s became a celebrated case of patriotic resistance to the West, and found its way into ukiyo-e prints, vernacular tales, and even into more learned "records" for intellectuals.[15] But subsequent inquiry into Kiyū's identity yielded nothing; she may have existed only in the minds of the Japanese who were eager to embrace just such a story.[16]

The faces of the prostitutes captured in the Beato-Stillfried studio evince the sadness of their lives. Some seem hardened and slatternly while others look shockingly young and bewildered (plates 26 and 27). Unlike the proud samurai with their challenging bright eyes, these women are all pensive and mute, as though looking into their own hopeless lot.

Yokohama Prints

The popular subgenres of "Yokohama prints" and "railroad prints" focused on precisely the Westernized elements that had been consciously excluded from tourist-oriented photographs. The same process of exclusion and distortion had been under way on the Japanese side as well, but in the reverse direction. Popular in the early 1860s, the "Yokohama prints" (which were for the most part designed and published in Edo) capitalized on the exoticism of the treaty port: foreign seamen hoisting sails; a bearded man walking with his wife in a ballooning skirt; the newly built racetracks for the Western residents; military musicians on Sunday parades; a large brick kitchen where women kneaded, men baked, children ran around, and dogs barked. Limited as they were, these images gave the Japanese masses their first glimpse into the Westerners' world (plates 28 and 29).

The "railroad prints," which replaced the "Yokohama prints" in popularity in the early 1870s, focused on the new Westernized aspects of Japan that were excluded from Yokohama photographs. The makers of the prints exploited the same commercial principle Yokohama photographers employed: provide the customers with what they want to see. What the Japanese sought, and found, in these prints was a glorified self-image, calculated to assuage any sense of inferiority vis-à-vis the West. The shabby reality was transformed into larger-than-life visions, in which stations soared like palaces, Japanese men and women stood tall in elegant Western clothes, and rows of gaslights illuminated treelined boulevards. The popularity of these fantasies reflects the insecurity the Japanese felt about the process of Westernization.

These tourist-oriented photographs of nineteenth-century Japan are thus one half of an ongoing dialogue between Western images of Japan and Japanese images of themselves—both constantly shifting to meet very different needs.

28. Utagawa Sadahide, 1871
Wood-block print (Courtesy The Harvard University Art Museums, Arthur M. Sackler Museum)

Sunday Procession in Yokohama

The technological and cultural transformations in Japan were infrequently documented through photography (which served a Western clientele with a taste for the exotic), but more often through wood-block prints produced for a Japanese audience.

29. Takeda Ilumaru, 1870s
Wood-block print (Courtesy Asian Art Museum of San Francisco, The Avery Brundage Collection)

Various Types of New Vehicles

NOTES

1. Interest in photography among various lords and scholars is discussed in detail in Nihon Shashinka Kyōkai, ed., *Nihon shashinshi 1840–1945*, pp. 353–356.

2. Daiichi Art Center, ed., *Shashin no makuake*, p. 148.

3. Ibid., p. 149.

4. Ibid., pp. 14–15.

5. The earliest dated reference to Beato in Yokohama was made by Wirgman in the article he sent to the *London News* on July 13, 1863. Wirgman mentioned that his house in Yokohama was crowded by the Japanese officials who wanted to see his sketches and his "companion Signor B..'s photographs." See Yokohama Kaikō Shiryōkan (Yokohama Archives), ed., *F. Beato Bakumatsu Nihon shashinshū*, p. 177.

6. Ibid., pp. 175–183.

7. Shimooka Renjō's various enterprises are documented on pp. 46–52 of *Suzuki Tsutoma, Bunmei kaika*.

8. Daiichi Art Center, ed., *Shashin no makuake*, p. 149.

9. Suzuki Tsutoma, *Bunmei kaika*, p. 51.

10. Daiichi Art Center, ed., *Shashin no makuake*, p. 149.

11. Pierre Loti, who arrived in Japan in the summer of 1885, witnessed the empress presiding over what probably was the first Western-style garden party in Japan, looking "resplendent in the latest Parisian fashion." Quoted in Linda Coverdale, trans., *Once Upon a Time*, p. 28.

12. *F. Beato Bakumatsu Nihon shashinshū*, p. 178.

13. Satow's friend in Japan, Dr. William Willis, indicated in his letter home that the majority of single Western males in the settlement are keeping one or two Japanese mistresses. See p. 147 of *Tōi gake* by Hagiwara Nobutoshi, the most recent biographical work on Ernest Satow.

14. Reference to *Yokohama Matsudaibanashi* can be found in Hijikata Sadaichi and Sakamoto Katsuhiko, eds., *Yokohama, Kobe*, p. 10.

15. An ukiyo-e print version, Toshinobu's "Shogi Kiyū no hanashi (1878)," is included in Hijikata Sadaichi and Sakamoto Katsuhiko, eds., *Yokohama, Kobe*, p. 10. The prose versions in *Kinsei kibun* (1874) by Somezaki Nobufusa and *Harusame bunko* (1876) by Matsumura Shunsuke are included on pp. 256–258 and pp. 309–314 of Okitsu Kaname, ed., *Meiji kaikaki bungakushū*.

16. See the biographical commentary on Yokohama characters in Hijikata Sadaichi and Sakamoto Katsuhiko, eds., *Yokohama, Kobe*, p. 157.

BIBLIOGRAPHY

Coverdale, Linda, trans.
1968 *Once Upon a Time*. New York: Friendly Press, Inc.

Daiichi Art Center, ed.
1985 *Shashin no makuake*. Vol. 1 of *Nihon shashin zenshū*. Tokyo: Shōgakukan.

Hagiwara, Nobuhisa
1980 *Tōi gake: Ernest Satow nikki-shō*, vol. 1. Tokyo: Asahi Shinbunsha.

Hijikata, Sadaichi and Sakamoto, Katsuhiko, eds.
1978 *Yokohama, Kobe*. Vol. 4 of *Meiji Taishō zushi*. Tokyo: Chikuma Shobō.

Miyoshi, Masao
1979 *As We Saw Them: The First Japanese Embassy to the United States (1860)*. Berkeley, Los Angeles, and London: University of California Press.

Nihon Shashin Kyōkai, ed.
1976 *Nihon shashinshi nenpyō 1778–1975.9*. Tokyo: Kōdansha.

Nihon Shashinka Kyōkai, ed.
1971 *Nihon shashinshi 1840–1945*. Tokyo: Heibonsha.

Okitsu, Kaname, ed.
1966 *Meiji kaikaki bungakushū*. Vol. 1 of *Meiji bungaku zenshū*. Tokyo: Chikuma Shobō.

Oliphant, Laurence
1860 *Narrative of the Earl of Elgin's Mission to China and Japan in the Years 1857, 1858, 1859*. New York: Harper and Brothers.

Satow, Ernest Mason
1921 *A Diplomat in Japan*. London: Seeley, Service and Co.

Suzuki, Tsutoma
1972 *Bunmei kaika*. Vol. 3 of *Nihonjin no hyakunen*. Tokyo: Sekai Bunkasha.

Yokohama Kaikō Shiryōkan (Yokohama Archives), ed.
1987 *F. Beato Bakumatsu Nihon shashinshū*. Yokohama Kaikōshiryō Fukyūkai.

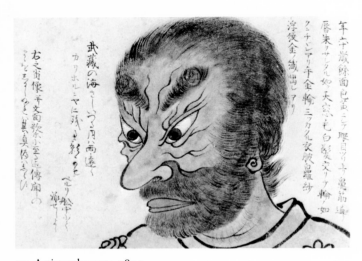

True Portrait of Perry, Envoy of the Republic of North America. His age is over 60. His face is sallow, eyes slanted, nose prominent. His lips are as though rouged. The hair on his head is partly white, and curly. . . . This portrait [is] here recorded simply as I was informed, and I cannot vouch for [its] accuracy.

ANONYMOUS ARTIST, 1854
from *The Black Ship Scrolls*

30. Artist unknown, 1853
Watercolor (Courtesy Honolulu Academy of Arts)

An anonymous Japanese artist's depiction of Commodore Perry, probably done from verbal description.

31, 32, 33. Artist unknown, 1853
Watercolor (Courtesy The Chrysler Museum, Norfolk, Va., Norfolk Newspaper's Art Trust, and in Memory of Donald W. Spark)

In this anonymous Japanese artist's depiction of Perry (far left) and his staff, faces are rendered individualistically and the uniforms carefully depicted.

Transition and the Quest for Permanence:
Photographers and Photographic Technology in Japan, 1854–1880s

BONNELL D. ROBINSON

This essay is concerned with photography, its uses and technology, at the time of and during the years following Commodore Matthew C. Perry's arrival in Japan in 1853 and 1854. Photographic procedures and processes invented in the mid-nineteenth century made photography vitally important to those who wanted the realism and credibility offered by the new technology. This was especially true of expeditionary photographers around the world who worked for governments or independently and sought to produce documentary evidence and convincing imagery. However, like artists, the motives and attitudes of Western and Japanese photographers in Japan greatly affected the kind of imagery they produced. Men from both cultures overcame technical and aesthetic challenges to express their respective visions of the newly opened country.

Photography and Related Image-Making in Japan at the Time of Perry's Arrival

The official introduction of photography into Japan coincided with an important event in nineteenth-century history: Commodore Perry's expedition to secure the first treaty between Japan and the United States. As was customary with expeditions of this kind, sketch-artists accompanied them to provide supporting visual materials. By 1853, photography was considered an equally valuable means of documentation. The importance Perry placed on his official photographer, Eliphalet Brown, Jr., and artist H. Heine, is clear from the special recognition he gives them in the intro-

duction to his three-volume illustrated book, *Narrative of the Expedition of an American Squadron to the China Seas and Japan*, compiled by Francis L. Hawks and published in 1856. Brown, who also did drawings during the trip, is credited with approximately 500 daguerreotypes as well. Heine depicted sensitive official negotiations between the Japanese and Americans, and Brown photographed everyday

life, landscapes, dress, and social and occupational types within Japanese society.

Japanese artists were as busy as the Americans documenting this historic encounter, whether making sketches or painting scrolls. Within the same culture we find varied interpretations. A number of scroll paintings now referred to as "the black ship scrolls" (the Japanese called Perry's squadron the "black ships of evil mien" when they were first seen in 1853), vary considerably in their depiction of their subjects. In one executed by an anonymous Japanese artist, Perry is represented as a demonic creature with fantastically distorted features and an orientalized face with an accompanying caption, "True portrait of Perry" (plate 30).[1] In a different painting of Perry and his official staff, another Japanese artist has rendered faces individualistically and delineated each uniform with care to depict dress and rank accurately[2] (plates 31, 32, 33).

34. Lithograph copied from daguerreotype by Eliphalet Brown, Jr., 1854
From Commodore Perry's *Narrative of Expedition to China Seas and Japan* (Courtesy Widener Library, Harvard University)

Japanese Priest in Full Dress, Simoda

Lithographs were copied from daguerreotypes taken by Eliphalet Brown, Jr., during Commodore Perry's expedition to Japan. In the lower left, note "Brown, Dag" indicating original maker of photograph. In lower right, "Richardson Cox, N.Y." names the copyist responsible for making a lithograph from the photograph.

Bonnell D. Robinson is Lecturer with Rank of Associate Professor of Fine Arts at Brandeis University and Associate Professor of Art History and Photography at the Art Institute of Boston.

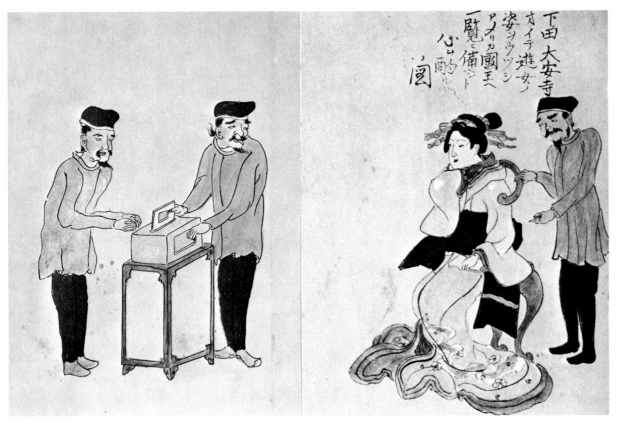

下田　大安寺
オイテ遊女ノ
姿ヲウツシ
アメリカ國王ヘ
一覧ニ備フト
心ゝ的ル
圖

35. Artist unknown, 1853
Watercolor (Courtesy The Japan Society)
In this portrayal of the daguerreotypist Eliphalet Brown, Jr., and his assistant (probably William Draper), an anonymous Japanese artist describes their effort to "record the appearance of a courtesan to show the American King."

Renderings by artists were based on subjective interpretation. Photographers, using a seemingly more authentic means of replication, were equally affected by personal motives and perceptions, cultural differences, and the medium in which they worked.

The Japanese had mixed reactions to the unfamiliar camera during this time. Although members of the scholarly elite wanted to learn the new process and the proud samurai, whose way of life was undergoing rapid transformation, wanted portraits made, contemporary sources indicate the camera was often viewed with suspicion and even fear. One account states that being photographed could cause the "shadow illness" or "shadow death": "Once photographed, your shadow will fade; Twice photographed, your life will shorten."[3] Eventually, increased familiarity with the camera led the Japanese to become one of the most camera-oriented countries in the modern world. As Matthew Perry observed:

The Japanese had all apparently a strong pictorial taste and looked with great delight upon the engravings and pictures that were shown them. . . . Every man . . . seemed anxious to try his skill at drawing and they were constantly taking the portraits of the Americans. . . .[4]

By the third quarter of the nineteenth century, Japanese photographers and their Western colleagues were producing some of the most accomplished photographic art and documentation in the history of the medium.

Early Photographers in Japan

Although photography had already made its way to Japan prior to Perry's expedition, Eliphalet Brown, Jr., is credited with making the first series of verifiable and exactly datable images and is still considered the first foreign photographer of consequence to document that country. Although almost all his daguerreotypes were destroyed by fire in the 1860s, many had already been converted into lithographs and woodcuts by skilled copyists after his return (plate 34). The next photographer of note from the West was J. G. Gower, an English diplomatic aide, who recorded the Japanese countryside and scenes of rural life. These photographs were copied and illustrated in his book, *Views of Japan*, in 1861. Aimé Humbert, Special Envoy and Minister to the Swiss Republic, traveled to Japan with his attaché, whose name is unknown but who was a competent artist and photographer.[5] They went beyond the boundaries set for foreigners around Yokohama to obtain information and views. After a stay of two years (1863–1864), Humbert published his volume in Paris as *Le Japon Illustré* in 1870. In his introduction, Humbert voiced a sentiment echoed by many others in reaction to the dramatic changes occurring in Japanese life and culture. His objective was to preserve "the strange life—art, manners and costumes—so graphically portrayed

... undergoing a rapid change, and soon [to be] a thing of the past."[6] In his book he based his illustrations not only on his own work but also on that of two acquaintances, Charles Wirgman and Felice Beato, as well as on a collection "of engravings, Indian-ink sketches, and colored pictures . . . of the Hidden scenes of Japanese life and history"[7] which he obtained from the print shops of Edo (Tokyo). Similar print shops would later sell the photographs done by both Western and Eastern cameramen to a primarily Western audience.

The two men most directly responsible for teaching photography to the Japanese were Felice Beato in the 1860s and the Baron Raimund Stillfried von Rathenitz in the following decade. Japan represented a new frontier to Beato, who had already documented half the globe as an expeditionary photographer. With James Robertson he had photographed the late stages of the Crimean War in 1854–1856 and documented the Indian Mutiny in 1857, after working in Constantinople, Athens, Egypt, and Palestine. In 1860, he continued to follow the advance troops of the British military eastward into China, where he made a realistic if gruesome record of the end of the Opium Wars. He arrived in Yokohama in 1863 at the suggestion of Wirgman, who had also been covering the Second Opium War as a correspondent. Beato lived and worked there until 1877. In the 1880s he went to Burma to sell furniture and native crafts in Mandalay and Rangoon, where he is reported to have died in 1906.

As an experienced and successful wet-plate photographer, especially adept at working in the field under the most trying conditions, Beato set extremely high standards for landscape, genre, architectural, and studio photography. These standards were maintained by Stillfried and his assistant, Kusakabe Kimbei. From 1865 to 1869, Beato and Wirgman ran a commercial studio together in Yokohama where they were a lively addition to the foreign community. Wirgman described the clientele during their early years:

... my house is inundated with Japanese officers who come to see my sketches and my companion Signor B——'s photographs. . . . Tomorrow the present regiment leaves and the officers of a new one just arrived have already paid us a visit.[8]

When Beato and Wirgman parted company in 1869, Beato set up his own studio under his own name and ran it until his competitor, Stillfried, purchased both studio and negatives on January 23, 1877. Stillfried, an Austrian, had traveled in the East before arriving in Yokohama in 1870 or 1871, when he established his studio under the name Stillfried & Co. The firm, which operated under the names of the Japanese Photographic Association and Stillfried & Andersen in 1875, continued until 1885. When Stillfried liquidated his stock, he sold a handsome portion to his former assistant, Kusakabe Kimbei, and the rest to A. Farsari, an entrepreneur who ran the largest photographic concern in Japan between the years 1886 and 1924. Both Kusakabe Kimbei and Farsari were located in Yokohama. Kusakabe Kimbei, considered one of the finest photographers in nineteenth-century Japan, ran a studio of his own from the 1880s to 1912. The firm of A. Farsari dealt in albums of views, particularly tinted views; many original photographs by Beato and Stillfried now bear the imprint of "A. Farsari," which introduces the problem of attribution.

Difficulties of Attribution

The difficulties of attribution now facing photographic historians of the period are considerable because almost all commercial photographers—Stillfried, Kusakabe Kimbei, Farsari, and others—followed a commonplace nineteenth-century practice of signing their own photographs as well as those purchased from other photographers. This difficulty is compounded by the succession of sales of stock not only to Stillfried by Beato in 1877, but also by Stillfried to Kusakabe Kimbei and the firm of A. Farsari around 1886. Once stock and negatives were

purchased, a photographer had the right to put his imprint on the photographs sold to the public. The tourist or collector who purchased an image identified as one by A. Farsari in 1888 might have received a photograph taken by Beato, Stillfried, or Kimbei.

In the twentieth century, concern for individual merit and credit makes it difficult to understand the seeming lack of concern on the part of these commercial photographers for what amounts today to plagiarism. At the time, however, photographs were a commodity, and purchasing stock meant buying the rights to it. Beato provides us with a good example of one man's attitude towards his photographic work. The fact that he made a remarkable record of the Near, Middle, and Far East did not, in his mind, necessarily mean only individual fame but also a life of adventure, subsidy for his photographic supplies, and ease in obtaining them as he followed the British military around the East. If the work was well done, technically and formally, it made his photography superior to that of his competitors, but it was still a documentary image to be used for commercial purposes. Thus the issue of authorship may have been inconsequential to Beato and others.

Another reason for the difficulty of attribution was the practice of making copy negatives of other photographers' work and attaching one's own name, rather than that of the original maker, to the prints made from these negatives. The popular portraits of Mutsuhito, the Emperor Meiji and his wife Haruko, the Empress of Japan are by Uchida Kuichi; however, two of the prints in this exhibition are mounted on Stillfried's embossed mattes (see plates 2, 36, 37). Another possibility the historian or cataloguer must consider is that the original photographer may have made a copy negative of his own print if the original glass-plate negative had been broken in handling or transporting.

To solve further problems of attribution, systematic comparisons need to be made between photographs and the most reliable sources, for example, the published edition of Felice Beato's book entitled *Photo-*

*[A] cloistered idol at whom the public was forbidden to look . . . . exquisite and extraordinary, with the
cool air of a goddess who looks out from within, gazing one knows not where.*

PIERRE LOTI,
from *Mukashi Mukashi*, 1984

36. Uchida Kuichi. Stillfried & Andersen Co. studio imprint, 1872
Albumen print (PM H15042)

Uchida Kuichi was commissioned to take portraits of the Emperor and Empress in 1872.

This photograph is on a Stillfried & Andersen matte with no reference to the original photographer's name. It was common practice for nineteenth-century photographers to take or purchase photographs and negatives from the stock of other studios and add their own names and negative numbers to the images.

37. Uchida Kuichi, 1872
Albumen print (WCM a1322)

Empress Haruko in ancient imperial costume.

This image does not bear the Stillfried & Andersen Co. studio imprint. Note the differences in detail and hand-coloring between plates 36 and 37.

graphic Views of Japan.[9] When comparisons of this nature cannot be made, it seems wise to remain open to the fact that attributions are best not given. A final identification of many of the images in this exhibition has been left open-ended out of respect for both photographers and scholarship in this area. No doubt, since research continues to be done in Japan, Europe, and the United States, new findings will provide answers to many of the questions still plaguing historians at this time.

Photographic Processes and Techniques

The first photographic process to reach Japan was the daguerreotype, invented by L. J. M. Daguerre in France in 1839. Dutch merchants were responsible for bringing a daguerreotype camera, equipment, and chemicals into Japan. The earliest surviving photograph made by a Japanese, dated 1857, is a portrait of the daimyo (feudal lord) of Satsuma, Shimazu Nariakira, who was one of photography's first patrons and amateur practitioners during the 1840s and early 1850s. The daguerreotype was a unique, direct-positive photograph on a highly reflective silver-coated plate of copper. Although difficult to view because of the mirrorlike surface, the image was sharp with precise detail and a long, subtle tonal scale.

By the early 1850s most serious photographers had begun to use the newly available wet-plate process invented by the Englishman Frederick Scott Archer in 1851. This process was so named because the emulsion of viscous collodion had to remain moist throughout the process of sensitizing, exposure, and development or the negative would fail to achieve the desired density in all areas. Some of the earliest examples of wet-plate negatives in Japan date from no later than 1853.[10] The major advantages of the wet-plate process were that an unlimited number of positive prints could now be made from a single glass-plate negative, and it had the same remarkable sharpness and an even longer tonal scale than the daguerreotype.

The wet-plate negative was eventually replaced by the more convenient dry-plate process, identical in almost every respect except that the emulsion did not have to remain moist; plates could be mass-produced and the photographer had the great advantage of developing the negative at his convenience. The dry-plate process became practical and commercially available by the mid-1870s. Another Englishman, Richard Kennett, introduced the dry-plate in 1873, and by 1878 Charles Harper Bennett had so improved the sensitivity of the emulsion that exposure times were dramatically shortened to a fraction of a second in the bright sun. This process would have arrived in Japan almost immediately after its invention; Beato and Stillfried would certainly have used both wet- and dry-plate negatives, whereas Kusakabe Kimbei may have used only the dry-plate process.

A fine printing paper is as important as a good negative, and the photographers in this exhibition had access to two of the most beautiful papers, which yielded the salt print and the albumen print. The wet-plate negative was printed on salt paper in the early years by some; however, the most popular paper was albumen, invented in 1850 by the Frenchman Louis Désiré Blanquart-Evrard, just prior to the invention of the wet-plate process. Albumen remained the paper of choice until almost 1900 and even later, although a third paper came into use in 1880, which yielded the silver gelatin print and is still used today. Some exceptionally fine examples of salt and albumen prints are included in this exhibition. The photographs made by Fredericks and Co. in New York City of some of the early Japanese delegates ca. 1860 are salt prints (plate 13). Despite the salt print's tendency to fade over time, a well-processed print has a particularly long, rich tonal range, which often leads people to believe the print is albumen. Almost all the images in this exhibition are albumen, and its characteristic look of lustrous tonalities has never been improved on and has rarely been equaled in photographic paper. The gloss of albumen also enhanced the contrast of the print since the sensitive silver salts were held on the surface of the paper in a thin emulsion of dried egg whites. This gloss is not as characteristic of salt prints because the fibers of the paper tend to absorb the sensitized solution, giving a more matte look. Photographers almost always toned albumen as its natural color was an undesirable green. Toning with gold chloride gave a range of possible tones from sepia-brown to purplish-black and tended to further stabilize the silver salts after fixing. A properly processed print from a good negative can look as beautiful today as it did a century ago (see plate 53).

The Studio and the Photographic Sitting

Commercial studios run by Japanese photographers began to open in the late 1850s and early 1860s. Among the best of these photographers were Shimooka Renjō in Yokohama, Ueno Hikoma in both Tokyo and Nagasaki, and Uchida Kuichi in Osaka and Yokohama. Next came the Westerners, Beato, who established his studio in Yokohama in 1863, followed by Stillfried, who began his commercial enterprise around 1871.

The formal studio had a comfortably furnished waiting room where the walls were usually covered with the photographer's best work. Clients consisted of diplomats and military men at first, then Western tourists and some Japanese. The client wanting a portrait would be shown into the photographic studio, positioned in front of a backdrop, plain or painted, and directed by the photographer until the right pose was found. The photographer or his assistant then left to prepare the collodion negative and, on returning, would check the sitter's pose and the lighting before making the exposure. The exposure time for a small carte-de-visite or a larger 8″ x 10″ plate varied from 30 to 120 seconds around 1851–1854 and from 1 to 60 seconds from 1864 until 1878, after which date times for a gelatin emulsion were 1/25 to 4 seconds. In some cases a head brace was required to keep movement in portraiture to an absolute minimum during longer exposures. Development of

38. Stillfried & Andersen Co. studio imprint, ca. 1860s–1870s
Albumen print (PM H15030)

An itinerant mender of smoking pipes.

This photograph has been attributed to Felice Beato. Beato may have been influenced by the *shajo*, an informal studio setting with a plain backdrop commonly used in Japan. Such a setting maximized the use of diffused northern light for shorter exposure times and allowed for a direct simple presentation.

the negative was done in an adjacent darkroom, usually by an assistant. The sitter remained in position until the negative had the final approval of the photographer.

The most informal kind of studio found in Japan during the last forty years of the nineteenth century was the simple *shajo*. Shajo might be found on streets near the busier sections of town and consisted of a backdrop hung from a tree or building, usually facing north to take advantage of evenly diffused light to prevent heavy shadows in the portrait. Foreigners or Japanese could spontaneously decide to have a photograph made, and the fee was considerably less than that charged by a conventional studio. Beato may have been inspired by the shajo to try some of his studio portraits and genre scenes outdoors against a simple blank backdrop (plate 38). By doing so he would have increased the amount of available natural light to shorten exposure times. In other instances he used the actual side of a building to give a feeling of authenticity to his photographs of street life.

The Darkroom

In the Bigelow and Knox collections are prints made from wet- or dry-plate collodion negatives. Many of the images were made with the more cumbersome wet-plate process, in which considerable manual dexterity was required to prepare, expose, and develop the negative before the moist emulsion dried. By necessity, the darkroom took many forms. It had to be large enough to work in, light-tight, and for the outdoor photographer, portable. In a conventional studio, the darkroom was adjoined for easy access. Photographers like Beato, Kusakabe Kimbei, and others who left the confines of the conventional studio for landscape or documentary work had to use a tent, wagon, or makeshift darkroom to sensitize plates and develop them before the collodion dried (plate 39).

In the wet-plate process, a glass plate had to be coated evenly with a viscous solution of collodion, which absorbed the light-sensitive silver salts when placed in a sensitizing bath. While still wet, the plate was put in the film holder, exposed in the camera for between 30 seconds to 2 minutes, depending on the size of the negative and amount of available light, then developed immediately.

The disadvantages of the process were in many respects its advantages. A photographer could examine the negative shortly after exposure and, if it were imperfect, make another exposure without revisiting the site or having to reconstruct the scene. Consequently, there was an extraordinary amount of quality work done by the demanding photographer.

The difficulties encountered because of the requirement for immediate development resulted in some remarkable solutions to the problem. Francis Frith in Egypt during the 1850s resorted to using the burial chambers of tombs for his darkroom, combating dust and bat droppings to prepare and develop his negatives.[11] Beato probably used a tent or converted wagon as darkroom on his expeditions. Because of his experience and expertise in outdoor photography, often under trying conditions, he no doubt made a significant number of landscape and documentary photographs in Japan, unlike Stillfried, who preferred the controlled atmosphere of the studio and a nearby darkroom.

Backgrounds, Compositions, and Stylistic Considerations

Backgrounds and compositions were important factors in the ultimate impact of an image. A variety of backgrounds were used for individuals or groups by the photographers in Japan. In many cases, Beato and Stillfried used simple backgrounds so as not to detract from the sitter's face, dress, or pose (plate 40). For interior genre scenes both men liked to include a few objects when appropriate to provide information about lifestyle or customs (plate 41).

39. Artist unknown, 1877
Wood engraving from *Les Merveilles de la Photographie* (Courtesy The Harvard University Art Museums, Arthur M. Sackler Museum)
European-style Portable Darkroom Tent
Photographers of the nineteenth century overcame the challenges of an unwieldy new technology. When working outside the studio, some transported a tent or make-shift darkroom, chemicals, and glass plates which had to be sensitized on the spot.

40. Studio unknown, ca. 1870s–1880s
Albumen print (PM H15040)

A man in formal robes.

This striking half-length portrait seems to typify Stillfried's preference for the tightly controlled studio situation.

41. Studio unknown, ca. 1870s–1880s
Albumen print (PM H15178)
Woman having her hair dressed.

The illusion of a particular setting was enhanced by the inclusion of furniture or objects related to the subject. This photograph has been attributed to Felice Beato.

The use of Western perspective in *Girls Reading a Letter* (plate 42) is meant to create a sense of the actual house in which the two women sit. The illustration of rooms receding in space behind the figures relieves the monotony of a flat foreground.

Life on the Ocean Wave includes an amusing background. Models are sitting in an unseaworthy-looking boat of small scale with painted waves breaking against the prow (plate 43). The juxtaposition of a badly painted Western picturesque setting with oriental subjects creates a forced and unintentionally humorous effect out of keeping with the works of Beato and Stillfried.

The practice of tinting albumen prints in Japan seems to have originated with Beato. Although familiarity with the tinted ukiyo-e prints may have inspired him, tinting of photographic prints was also widely practiced in the West. Beato was fortunate, however, to find among the artisan class tinters who colored a variety of goods, among them silks. Plate 44 shows a tinter at work on a small print or photograph. In *Photographic Views of Japan*, Beato pays homage to his colorist with a full-length portrait. Stillfried and Kusakabe Kimbei also followed the high standards of hand-tinting. Two reasons that the quality of tinting in Japan was so remarkable were that the colorists were well-trained and the Japanese used water-soluble tints, which gave greater translucency than the oil pigments which predominated in the West.

Beato's aims remained largely documentary, and his interests were varied: portraits of types, genre scenes, landscapes, aspects of Japanese life. Stillfried was more consciously artistic in his approach to subject matter. His emphasis on the individual portrait and use of the close-up was an innovation in the East at this time. Unlike Beato and Kusakabe Kimbei, he had less interest in documentary work. In his choice of subjects and carefully crafted compositions, Stillfried pursued his own ideal of oriental beauty and perfection (see plate 21). The more personal aesthetic approach of Stillfried is in distinct contrast to the more naturalistic approach of Beato (plate 38).

42. Kusakabe Kimbei, ca. 1870s–1880s
Albumen print (PM H15075, Gift of W. A. Dunn)

Girls Reading a Letter

Western perspective was used in most painted backgrounds for studio portraits during this period. In this example, the backdrop creates the illusion of receding rooms. This image appears in a catalogue that Kusakabe Kimbei prepared to advertise his inventory.

43. Kusakabe Kimbei, ca. 1880s
Albumen print (PM H15088, Gift of Dr. George B. Gordon)

Life on the Ocean Wave

Here oriental models are juxtaposed with a badly rendered Western picturesque setting.

44. Studio unknown, ca. 1870s–1880s
Albumen print (PM H 1 5 1 4 2)

Japanese colorist at work.

Beato initiated a tradition of hand-coloring photographs
in Japan. Tinting was frequently executed by artists trained
in coloring wood-block prints.

Like the Japanese and American artists who first
depicted each other in 1853, nineteenth-century photographers had many options relating to materials,
techniques, choice of subject, and stylistic controls to
convey their vision of a place and people. The camera,
for all its potential realism, sees what the photographer intends. That these men were commercial photographers does not mean their only motive was
financial gain. They did not take their responsibility
as documentarians or artists lightly, as we can see
from the exceptionally fine work they did while in
Japan. Their quest to preserve a culture in transition
is characterized by a sensitivity to their subject, an
eagerness to find creative and artistic ways of ap-
proaching their task, and a commitment to their individual interpretations of Japan, which resulted in a
unique contribution to the history of photography.

NOTES

1. Oliver Statler, *The Black Ship Scroll*, p. 34.
2. George Henry Preble, *The Opening of Japan*, p. 326.
3. Japan Photographers Association, *A Century of Japanese Photography*, p. 7.
4. Francis L. Hawks, *Narrative of the Expedition of an American Squadron*, p. 147.
5. Aimé Humbert, *Le Japon Illustré*, p. iii.
6. Aimé Humbert, *Japan and the Japanese* (an English translation of *Le Japon Illustré*), pp. v–vi.
7. Ibid., p. vi.
8. Charles Wirgman, *The London Illustrated News*, July 1863.
9. Felice Beato, *Photographic Views of Japan*. Beato's book consisted of two albums, "Views of Japan" and "Native Types." Other related albums by Beato exist but without the full number of plates (98 and 100 in each of the two volumes respectively) and without the proper frontispiece. Beato or his firm made these less expensive albums with fewer plates, for tourists who wanted to make their own selections.
10. Japan Photographers Association, *A Century of Japanese Photography*, p. 7.
11. Francis Frith, *Egypt and the Holy Land in Historic Photographs*, p. xiv.

BIBLIOGRAPHY

Beato, Felice
1868 *Photographic Views of Japan with Historical and Descriptive Notes, Compiled from Authentic Sources, and Personal Observation During a Residence of Several Years.* 2 vols. Yokohama.

Benjamin, Sol
1983 "Views of Japan: Photographs by Felix Beato." *Aperture Magazine* 90.

Cameron, M. E., Thomas H. D. Maloney, and George E. McReynolds
1960 *China, Japan and the Powers.* 2nd. ed. New York: Ronald Press.

Crawford, William
1979 *The Keepers of Light: A History and Working Guide to Early Photographic Processes.* New York: Morgan and Morgan, Dobbs Ferry.

Frith, Francis
1980 *Egypt and the Holy Land in Historic Photographs: 77 Views by Francis Frith.* New York: Dover Publications Inc.

Gernsheim, Helmut, and Alison Gernsheim
1969 *The History of Photography: From the Camera Obscura to the Beginning of the Modern Era.* New York: McGraw-Hill Book Co.

Gower, J. G.
1861 *Views of Japan.* London: Negretti and Zambra.

Hawks, Francis L.
1856 *Narrative for the Expedition of an American Squadron to the China Seas and Japan, Performed in the Years 1852, 1853, and 1854, under the Command of Commodore M. C. Perry, U. S. Navy, by Order of the Government of the United States.* Compiled from the original notes and journals of Commodore Perry and his officers, at his request and under his supervision, by Francis L. Hawks. New York: D. Appelton and Co.

Humbert, Aimé
1870 *Le Japon Illustré.* Paris: L. Hachette et Cie.
1874 *Japan and the Japanese.* Translated by Mrs. Cashel Hoey. Edited by H. W. Bates. London: Richard Bentley and Son.

Japan Photographers Association
1980 *A Century of Japanese Photography.* Introduction by John W. Dower. New York: Pantheon Books, Random House.

Pare, Richard
1982 *Photography and Architecture, 1839–1939.* Montreal: Canadian Centre for Architecture.

Preble, George Henry
1962 *The Opening of Japan: A Diary of Discovery in the Far East.* Norman: University of Oklahoma Press.

Reischauer, Edwin O., and Albert M. Craig
1978 *Japan: Tradition and Transformation.* Boston: Houghton Mifflin Co.

Statler, Oliver
1963 *The Black Ship Scroll: An Account of the Perry Expedition at Shimodo in 1854 and the Lively Beginnings of People-to-People Relations between Japan and America,* trans. Richard Lane; scroll paintings in full color by an Anonymous Japanese Eyewitness. A Weathermark Edition privately printed for the Japan Societies of San Francisco and New York.
1969 *Shimoda Story.* New York: Random House.

Wirgman, Charles
1863 *The London Illustrated News,* July.

Worswick, Clark
1979 *Japan: Photographs 1854–1905.* Introduction by Jan Morris and A. Pennwick. New York: Alfred A. Knopf.

45. Studio unknown, ca. 1870s–1880s
Albumen print (WCM A1311)

A young woman in a posture of sleep.

Tradition, Novelty, and Invention:
Portrait and Landscape Photography in Japan, 1860s–1880s

ELLEN HANDY

Although new to Japan, the photographic art practiced by Europeans there from the 1860s onwards already had a history of more than twenty years in Europe, where it also formed part of the enormously longer history of Western image-making. Early European photographic artists in Japan, such as the Venetian Felice Beato and the Austrian Baron Raimund Stillfried von Rathenitz, were at once the explorers of what was to them an uncharted land and uninvited visitors to a complex society and elaborate culture. Their pictures are the result of the remarkable synthesis of their own artistic traditions and assumptions about photography, their fascinating and alien subject matter, and the invention and ingenuity that mediated between these elements. While the inventiveness of these photographers is expressed in the solutions they found to the pictorial problems that arose in their work, their general approach was to rely on familiar techniques and conventions of their young but established art to record and express the breadth, detail, and staggering novelty of the society in which they had immersed themselves.

Those conventions had inevitably grown out of existing ideas about how to represent the world in pictures and about what—and who—should be depicted. Those ideas, of course, were those of painters, printmakers, and draughtsmen. In Western secular art of the latter part of the nineteenth century, portrait, landscape, and still life were three of the most important genres or categories in which artists might work, and each of these was immediately adopted by photographers seeking to represent the world with their

newly invented medium. Each of the genres had its own history, rules, and patterns of meaning. Of these, portraiture and landscape were tremendously important in Japan, representing the majority of photographs produced there, as elsewhere in the world.

Tradition and Invention

The Western genres of travel portraiture and landscape were heir to a plentiful and varied endowment of artistic traditions. The traveling portraitist either based his picture on some familiarity with the subject or was forced to rely upon a system of conventions for depicting people, which became a sort of portrait methodology to be learned and followed by rote in each situation. Given that the degree of intimacy between subject and artist was crucial in determining the content and nature of the portrait, in the case of portraitists working in a foreign land a particular kind of distance was interposed between subject and artist. The pose, gestures, and expressions considered appropriate to a photograph constituted a pictorial framework that could be imposed indiscriminately and then modified by the artist's perceptions concerning the approximate social status and identity of individual subjects.

Makers of Western landscape pictures also relied on pre-established models. From the eighteenth century through the middle of the nineteenth century European and American artists made *le grand tour*, sketching the picturesque and contemplating the sub-

lime in the works of both man and nature across Europe, into the Middle East, and beyond. If portrait photographers could look to Rembrandt and Ingres as models for psychological insight and brilliant accuracy of rendering in portraiture, respectively, then Canaletto and Turner might serve as exemplars for the landscape photographer who sought through composition to subjectively interpret the landscape as an aesthetic and symbolic space.

Photography's unique capability of recording reality in complete, instantaneous, and convincing detail gave it a reportorial authority that painting and drawing lacked, and hence assigned it the documentary application of recording information of the most basic kind. A product of the technology of modern European society, photography was both the most efficient tool for depicting the process of Japan's penetration by both the representatives and the culture of the industrialized West, and itself a part of that culture and of that penetration.

By the 1860s a photographer at work amid a foreign culture could draw from a growing body of photographic techniques and conventions. Portrait photographers in Europe, such as Adolphe Disderi of Paris, had developed mass-production strategies for portraiture by means of which people could be "processed" as photographic subjects very quickly, reducing each to an almost undifferentiated formula and product. Similarly in the landscape field, topographic specialists such as the British firm Frith & Co. systematically covered a given region, composing each town, site, and landmark as a picturesque view ac-

Ellen Handy is Research Assistant in the Department of Prints and Photographs at The Metropolitan Museum of Art, New York, and a Ph.D. candidate in the history of photography at Princeton University.

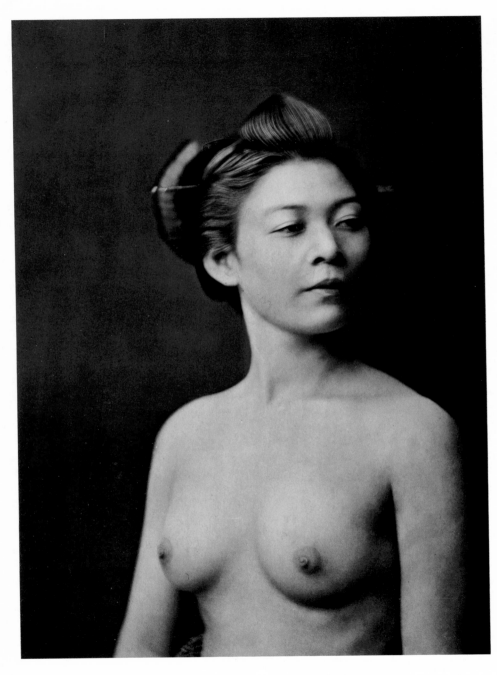

cording to classically derived compositional principles.

While photographers often relied upon fixed, formulaic approaches to new terrain and cultural experiences, those who first worked in Japan tended to be exceptions to this rule. Among exotic cultures sought out by Europeans and Americans in the latter half of the nineteenth century, Japan was a particularly complex, purposely isolated society which possessed a thriving and sophisticated graphic tradition and art market. The unfamiliar beauties of the Japanese terrain yielded thousands of landscape views, and the unfamiliar physiognomic and other characteristics of the people similarly were recorded again and again. Some of the subject matter of Japan was, however, so unprecedented in the experience and understanding of the photographers that it significantly affected the pictorial form in which the content was expressed by causing the photographers to expand or to alter their conventions.

Camera Artists in Japan
and Their Pictures

In some of the photographs of Stillfried and others, there is a sense of dialogue, more the making of a photograph than the taking of it. That photographs are *made* is a crucial idea, for it reflects the elements of intention, interpretation, selection, improvisation, and deception that are part of the process. We have come to realize that despite its marvelous detail and apparent mirroring of an objective reality, each photograph is a fiction and an artifice. Photographs can and do lie, but more importantly, more subtly misleading, they edit, alter, eliminate, and interpret in

46. Stillfried & Andersen Co. studio imprint, ca. 1860s–1870s
Albumen print (PM H14993)

A prostitute.

Western photographers often staged Japanese women at their toilette, asleep, or seminude.

47. Stillfried & Andersen Co. studio imprint, ca. 1867–1868
Albumen print (PM H I 5060)

Decapitation and display of the severed head was a common form of punishment in pre-modern Japan.

The image is presented in a calmly reportorial fashion that suggests the work of Beato, who was well-known for his graphic photographs from the battlefields of the Crimea and China. This print, which is mounted on a Stillfried & Andersen matte, presumably represents an example of the studio's practice of attaching their own imprint to Beato's stock.

ways that are not immediately apparent. The seeming precision and accuracy of all that we see within the image makes us forget what is outside it, including the photographer and camera. Photographs are most insidious in their deception, and most insistent in their interpretation, when they seem most direct, transparent, and "true."

The artifice is quite evident, for instance, in Stillfried's photographs of young Japanese women. In scenes of domestic activity, the women are gracefully arranged like still-life elements; photographs of their actual work probably would have been less legible and concise as description, even if more authentic as documentation. Other pictures include precisely staged depictions of women's toiletry and sleeping arrangements, and half-length portraits of young women with their draperies neatly but implausibly adjusted to reveal one or both of their breasts (plates 45 and 46). The coy seminudity tells us more about the photographer and audiences than about the customs of Japanese women. These photographs are a local variation on the mainstream of Western images of courtesans and seductive women from Titian's *Venus* and Manet's *Olympia* to the erotic photographs and nude studies made by European photographers for artistic and recreational purposes. Such photographs as these document the Western artists' fantasy of the excitingly alien, sexually pliant Eastern woman; they belong as well to a more specialized tradition in Western art that concerns itself with the exotic aspects of Middle Eastern or oriental cultures. As such these photographs owe more to Delacroix's or Ingres's intensely imagined seraglio scenes than they do to an objective reality in Japan.

Problems of attribution make it difficult to analyze the precise extent of the compromises and conflicts between Western and Eastern pictorial traditions. Largely because of the transfer of negatives among Western and Japanese photographers, it is not clear whether several artists share a given characteristic, or where a characteristic is indicative of a single photographer's style. Without firm attributions, one cannot

48. Stillfried & Andersen Co. studio imprint, ca. 1860s–1870s
Albumen print (PM H15031)

A traveling tinker.

This photograph has been attributed to Felice Beato, much of whose work documented social and occupational types.

offer complete art-historical interpretations of isolated images, whose meaning would be profoundly extended by knowledge of the identity of the artist, his history and practice.

As the preceding essays have noted, Felice Beato was the first Western photographer to work extensively in Japan. He established a pattern of traveling to remote eastern regions where current events created opportunities for timely and exotic photographs for the European market, which makes it tempting to see much of his work as prototypical photojournalism. Yet the pictures he made are as often landscape or architectural views as reportage.[1] The methodology of the picturesque tour informed Beato's view-making, complementing his canny instinct for sensational locations and situations. Even in his most shocking Japanese subjects, such as the public display of severed heads, he applies the standard compositional procedures he had developed in his battlefield scenes in the Crimea and China (plate 47). His calmly reportorial tone is somewhat disingenuously combined with an evident fascination for the macabre qualities of the picture.

In general, Beato's *Photographic Views of Japan* is at once more sedate and more exhaustive than his work from other countries. Instead of battles and ruins, he inventoried the social and occupational types he found in the streets of Yokohama, and catalogued the landscape as far as he was allowed to travel outside the city (plate 48). This subject material, somewhat atypical for Beato, was closer to the work of other photographers, like Stillfried.

Stillfried was born in Austria where he studied painting and served as an officer in the army. He traveled to China and America before reaching Japan in 1870, when his first photographic studio, Stillfried & Co., was established in Yokohama, the center also of Beato's operations.[2] Stillfried worked in photography for seven years before acquiring Beato's negatives and studio. He successfully ran his studios, including Stillfried & Andersen and the Japan Photographic Association, until 1883 when he returned to

Vienna. Kusakabe Kimbei, who is assumed to have been active in Stillfried's studio as apprentice, camera operator, or associate, bought most of the stock of the Japan Photographic Association and Stillfried & Co., and continued to be active in photography until 1912.[3] The remainder of Stillfried's stock was purchased by A. Farsari & Co., who became well-known for issuing albums of landscape views in great quantity, but without regard for print quality and delicacy of hand-coloring. Stillfried is in some ways the most important figure in this exhibition because there is positive identification of many of the images as coming from his studio, if not necessarily from his camera. Stillfried is at the center of the interwoven careers of Beato, Kusakabe Kimbei, and A. Farsari & Co., and more closely connected to each of them than they are to each other.

Portraits

Stillfried's portraits are often more elegant than bold, more subtle than striking. The fine quality and delicacy of their hand-coloring by his colorists is exceptional. His portraits are studied rather than spontaneous and have all the concentration and deliberation characteristic of pictures made within the restricted but specialized environment of the studio. Working this way narrowed Stillfried's horizons, especially when compared to Beato, but allowed him to perfect his portrait style. His portraits have two functions, serving as both artistic studies and commercial products, conveying great elegance in either role. As the demand for portraits increased on the part of the Japanese public, the commercialism and high style of Stillfried's work became important locally as well as in terms of the tourist export trade. His polished style is particularly unlike that of Beato, whose casual and animated figures are illustrative of social types more than they are portraits focusing on the inherent qualities of an individual.

The beauty and restraint of Stillfried's style is often to be seen in his omission of extraneous props and furnishings, and the simplicity of his compositions. One fine portrait of a samurai in a blue robe is clearly a studio picture, but a few pebbles arranged on the rough cloth that enfolds the base of a potted plant and covers the floor suggests the out-of-doors with great refinement and economy of means (plate 49). The deftness and artifice with which the stones and plant imply rather than indicate landscape can be compared with the compression of poetic metaphor. A portrait probably attributable to Stillfried of a blind masseur with staff and flute, posed beside a stone lantern in the studio, is a contemplative study of a rather distant character as much as it is an illustration of a profession. The masseur's blindness and his placement in the artificial studio setting make for a remote and self-contained image (see plate 7). While Stillfried's portraits carefully and respectfully render the appearance of individual sitters, they are by no means psychological studies, as they have sometimes been interpreted. The personalities of these men behind their physiognomy remain unknown to the viewer; the art of the pictures lies more in the grace of depiction than in the interpretation of character.

Stillfried's portrait of a young woman wearing European jewelry with her Japanese coiffure and bare shoulders in a sense is a character study, but not an intimate or anecdotal one (plate 50). Whether the photographer chose to adorn his model in Western ornaments or whether they were perhaps gifts of a European lover is impossible to tell. It is the contrast of adornment and bared skin with the proudly reserved gaze of the woman that gives the picture its strength.

The minimalism of some of Stillfried's portraits appeals to our contemporary tastes, which on the whole are more tolerant of austerity than were those of the nineteenth century. It allows the viewer to concentrate upon the sheer novelty of subjects like the two massive sumo wrestlers in full embrace, who are depicted in the plainest possible studio setting. Al-

49. Studio unknown, ca. 1870s–1880s
Albumen print (WCM a1331)
Samurai.

Stillfried's portraiture is at its finest in those pictures that both acknowledge and
transcend the limits of the studio. In this picture, perhaps by Stillfried, reference is
made to the outdoors although it is clearly a studio portrait.

50. Stillfried & Andersen Co. studio imprint, ca. 1860s–1870s
Albumen print (PM H14991)

A prostitute.

This studio portrait shows a woman in a Western pose wearing European jewelry.

though posed, they convey the stresses and force of the actual wrestling bout (plate 51).

Not all of Stillfried's portraits display the simplicity that is so highly prized today. Like all commercial portraitists of his time, he possessed a stock of studio props and backdrops with which to augment his compositions. It is possible that Stillfried himself preferred to work in the plainer style of the pictures described above, but it is also possible that he merely considered it an alternative to the typically ornate portraits in which figures pose before illusionistically painted landscapes and other settings. One example of such a portrait depicts three young women in kimonos standing before a wooded scene painted in the Western manner of the Barbizon school (plate 52). The conflict of East and West is manifested in the pronounced incompatibility of the style of the naturalistic background scene with that of the figures. The awkwardness is increased by the unnatural positioning of the women, who stand very close together without making eye contact with one another.

Stillfried's greatest contribution to photography lay in his ability to apply his photographic technology and the sophistication of the Western portrait tradition to a novel Eastern subject matter. The tensions arising from this application are sometimes present even where the crude backdrops are not used, as for instance in a half-length portrait of two girls (plate 53). They are shown in profile, leaning together, one with her arms around the other's neck. The pose reflects an insistence upon the Western image of girl-

51. Stillfried & Andersen Co. studio imprint, ca. 1860s–1870s
Albumen print (PM H15046)

Sumo wrestlers.

Given the absence of detail in the background, attention is fully focused on the sumo wrestlers, whose pose suggests the forces and stresses of an actual wrestling bout.

hood that almost entirely dominates the sitters. The portrait owes more to the repertoire of packaged poses of the Western commercial photographer or painter than to the observation of Japanese girls' attitudes and gestures. Stillfried de-contextualizes the subjects rather imperiously; he does not allow the sitters to determine their own image. Nevertheless, he does attend faithfully to their individuality, composing them with dignity and grace. This image, then, is most telling as a portrait of the girls' place within an Eastern society under pressure from the West.

Although Stillfried's various studios were among the most successful in nineteenth-century Japan, the proliferation of Japanese photographers provided competition for him as for other Europeans. There were some arenas in which the foreigners could not compete. Imposing portraits of Mitsuhito, the Emperor Meiji, and his wife Haruko (both of 1872) were made by Uchida Kuichi, in imperial commission not extended to the European photographers (plates 2, 36, 37).[4] The emperor is arrayed in Western military attire while the empress appears in traditional dress. He is seated in a heavy chair placed on a patterned carpet of European design, while she stands on an oriental rug spread over the same carpet seen in her husband's portrait. Both pictures seem very Western, bearing a similarity to contemporary portraits of Western heads of state and aristocrats, which in turn resemble portraits of ordinary members of the bourgeoisie.

52. Stillfried & Andersen Co. studio imprint, ca. 1860s–1870s
Albumen print (PM H15017)
Three geishas holding hands in the manner of a sentimental, Victorian group portrait.

The landscape photographs in this exhibition present quite different problems and questions than do the portraits. The problems of attribution are even more acute than in the case of the portraits since even the mark of Stillfried's studio is lacking. Some landscape views presented here may well have been taken from Beato's negatives, which could have been printed and sold by Beato, Stillfried, or even Farsari, but other photographers may also have been involved. It is not known whether Stillfried himself ever ventured outside his studio to photograph landscapes—his style seems to be best suited to studio work. He may have relied upon Beato's negatives for landscape views, or he may have sent his assistants to photograph in the country. Kusakabe Kimbei is known to have made many landscapes, probably both during and after his time in Stillfried's studio.

The landscape view was at least as important in Japanese art of the nineteenth century as it was in occidental art of the period, so indigenous models were available for foreign photographers to follow as they began photographing the Japanese landscape. These examples consisted not only of existing landscape pictures and styles, but of the landscape idea, the identification of particular important sites as being in themselves "views" or "landscapes." It is, after all, not merely the configuration of topography that makes a landscape, but also associations, assumptions and the investment of meaning. By the 1860s, when photographers began to work exten-

53. Stillfried & Andersen Co. studio imprint, ca. 1860s–1870s
Albumen print (PM H15009)

Two young women in a conventional Western pose.

The sentimentality of this photograph belongs to Western social and artistic conceptions of girlhood. Despite the relative dignity and grace of the subjects, the photographer's imposition of Western ideas and pose dominates the sitters.

54. Studio unknown, ca. 1870s–1880s
Albumen print (WCM a1389)

Garden of Palace, Tokyo

A view of a characteristically Japanese subject like this garden can be represented using the same principles of composition that Western artists first developed during the Renaissance for the depiction of Western scenes. Oriental in subject, the photograph is occidental in style and pictorial method.

No object is more visited near Yokohama by excursions than the bronze statue of Daibouts [sic].

FELICE BEATO, 1868
Photographic Views of Japan

56. Studio unknown, ca. 1870s–1880s
Albumen print (WCM a1357)

Rice Plantation

Photographers using Japanese compositional techniques of broad planes and graphic delineation participated in a complex process of stylistic interactions between Eastern and Western pictorial traditions.

55. Studio unknown, ca. 1870s–1880s
Albumen print (WCM a1354)

Daibutsu

This presentation of the monumental Buddha sculpture at Kamakura is a good example of a straight-forward travel view whose purpose was simply to record a single subject or location. The subject takes precedence over the image and its pictorial qualities.

MEGANE-BASHI. 399.

57. Studio unknown, ca. 1870s–1880s
Albumen print (WCM A1351)

Megane—Bashi. A "spectacles bridge" in Tokyo over a lotus pond.

One characteristic of Japanese art that appealed to Westerners, and that could be employed in photography, was the juxtaposition of objects in different size scales, suggesting distance. Here, the unexpected juxtaposition of waterlilies and figures emphasizes the photograph's abstract elements of shape and pattern.

RED LACQUERED BRIDGE AT NIKKO.

58. Studio unknown, ca. 1870s–1880s
Albumen print (WCM a1380)

Red Lacquered Bridge at Nikko

Japanese compositions seldom show the plunging vistas of exploratory photographic landscapes of the nineteenth century. In this picture of a frequently depicted motif, the bridge is seen from the side as in Japanese prints, serving as a barrier in the center of the landscape rather than a path to follow or a means of crossing from one point to another.

59. Kusakabe Kimbei, ca. 1880s
Albumen print (WCM a1302)

A Buddhist procession.

This now well-known photograph by Kusakabe Kimbei shows his interest in everyday customs and life in Japan, his high standards for color tinting, and his subtle marshaling of space in terms that do not correspond to photographic conventions or Western perspective.

sively in Japan, Japanese artists had already identified many of the great picturesque views of the countryside, particularly around Mt. Fuji and on the Tō-kaidō, the great highway between the old capital of Kyoto and the new one of Tokyo, close to Yokohama. Wood-block landscape prints made by artists such as Hokusai and Hiroshige traced the routes travelers followed to see the views firsthand. These artists so brilliantly codified scenes in the Japanese landscape that it must have been difficult for photographers to see other than through the printmakers' eyes. The influence of the Japanese prints upon the Europeans' photographs is felt most strongly in the coloring of photographs in the manner of prints by highly skilled Japanese colorists. The intricacy of the network of influences is great, for Hokusai's innovative style of composition represents his absorption of western one-point perspective—an alternative to the flattened planes of oriental art—and other artistic conventions which he encountered in Dutch prints toward the end of the eighteenth century, before Western culture became widely known in Japan. While his highly stylized compositions look extremely un-Western to Western eyes, they represent a crucial first phase of the cultural transference that doubled back upon itself when Western photographers and other artists discovered his work and assumed it to be uniquely Japanese. When we consider the phenomenon of Japanese photographers studying landscape composition under Western artists who were so immersed in oriental view and images, the cross-fertilization of ideas and styles seems complete.

Landscape photographs could also fulfill a simpler function than that of the prints. The great demand for informative photographs to serve as mementos for visitors to Japan, and as edification and entertainment for an audience far away, ensured the production of many photographs like the view of the great Buddha in the temple garden (plate 55). These pictures tended to be composed in as straightforward a fashion as possible.

Views that sought instead, through camera angle and perspective, to arrange topographic elements into pleasing pictures were common as well. In plate 54 the decorative garden view with a lantern in the foreground and a lake in the central zone of the picture is organized quite comfortably in Western spatial and pictorial terms so that the eye is free to move back and forth through successive planes of the landscape. *Rice Plantation* depicts a line of stooped workers with wide round hats in a rice paddy (plate 56). The handling of the delicately linear rice shoots in the water and the frieze of workers borrow from the compositions of printmakers like Hiroshige. In the foreground of *Megane-Bashi*, a profusion of large lily pads seems to push the bridge and the people on it firmly into the background (plate 57). The lily pads come to dominate the scene because of their emphatic pattern and the low camera angle that exaggerates their size. The predomination of the foreground over the nominal content of the scene, the bridge, indicates that the image is primarily an aesthetic rendering rather than a documentary transcription.

Foreground elements that dominate a picture may also block the eye's progress into the heart of the landscape. Exploratory photographic landscapes of the nineteenth century were frequently made from commanding positions that allowed deep vistas into the terrain, a characteristic as much symbolic of penetration and domination as revealing of scenery. Japanese compositions, traditionally much shallower than Western ones and reliant upon multiple points of view, resist this compositional impetus. In the *Red Lacquered Bridge at Nikko*, the space behind the bridge is closed, and successive planes of distance do not give way to each other in an accessible progression toward the horizon (plate 58). The landscape keeps its secrets, revealing only the picturesque charm of the bridge; it does not invite the viewer to enter, implicitly reminding us of the restrictions placed on travel by foreigners within the interior of the country.

It took the emergence of a truly Japanese photog-

raphy to produce images that had Japanese subjects rather than Western expectations as their true content. One striking example from these collections is a photograph made by Kusakabe Kimbei of a Buddhist procession (plate 59). The sea of faces, each with attention riveted on the camera, fills the frame of the photograph. The collagelike multiplicity of detail is disconcerting. The people are posed as precisely as an arrangement of still-life elements, but their great number makes them appear more like the rocks on the mountain or the trees in the forest of a landscape. Without the coloring that distinguishes the ceremonial red umbrellas, the robes of the priests, and other details, the great mass of the crowd would be pictorially unmanageable. Spatial organization is important only for the purpose of including as many participants in the procession in the picture as possible. The railing to the right of the crowd and the receding line of umbrellas at its center organize the space, and the slope on which the procession has halted works like the pitch of a theater floor, bringing all of the heads into one line of vision. But the steep path on which the people stand is scarcely visible beneath them, so they seem to float contrary to logic and perspective.

Kusakabe Kimbei's arresting photograph subtly marshals space without relying on photographic conventions or Western perspective that would rationalize the recession of space. The familiarity of a Japanese photographer with such a subject gives a certain intimacy to the picture, yet the interruption of the procession which resulted in this motionless moment was imposed by the photographer with more regard for the camera than for custom. With a picture such as this, Japanese photography began to come of age as Japanese artists took into their own hands the tools of photography and the teachings of foreigners like Beato or Stillfried, to invent new pictorial forms for their own experience and expression.

NOTES

1. Italo Zannier, *Antonio e Felice Beato*.
2. *Geschichte der Fotografie in Österreich*, Band II, Bad Isch, 1983, p. 184.
3. Clark Worswick, *Japan Photographs 1854–1905*, p. 135.
4. *Ibid*.

BIBLIOGRAPHY

Beato, Felice
1868   *Photographic Views of Japan with Historical and Descriptive Notes, Compiled from Authentic Sources, and Personal Observation During a Residence of Several Years*. 2 vols. Yokohama.

Edel, Chantal
1984   *Mukashi Mukashi: The Japan of Pierre Loti 1863–1883*. Photographs by Felice Beato and Raimund von Stillfried. Paris: Arthaud.
1983   *Geschichte der Fotografie in Österreich*, Band II, Bad Isch.

Loti, Pierre
1910   *Madame Chrysanthème*. New York: Current Literature Co.

Worswick, Clark
1979   *Japan Photographs 1854–1905*. Introduction by Jan Morris and A. Pennwick. New York: Alfred A. Knopf.

Zannier, Italo
1983   *Antonio e Felice Beato*. Venice: Ikon Photo Gallery.

60. Studio unknown, ca. 1870s–1880s
Albumen print (WCM a1307)
Women enjoying the cherry blossoms from rickshaws.

The exploratory and travel photography of the nineteenth century was a curious hybrid of pictorial representation and historical documentation, and an expression of the expeditionary spirit. The negatives brought back from Japan yielded prints that were part of the spoils to which the explorers or visitors felt entitled, much like the archaeological relics, local handicrafts, and indigenous flora and fauna that were also collected, removed from their contexts, classified, and often publicly exhibited. They served the additional purpose of stimulating the curiosity of those who were not able to travel to distant places themselves, but who might enjoy and learn from these foreign realms vicariously through the photographs. With the passage of time, their continued examination reveals a surprising wealth of meaning, which continues to clarify our thinking about the cultural dialogue between East and West.

61. Stillfried & Andersen Co. studio imprint, ca. 1860s–1870s
Albumen print (PM H15026)
Two performers in a skit or dance. One performer holds a pipe and tobacco pouch.